ON
HER WAY

The Shania Twain Story

Scott Gray

BALLANTINE BOOKS • NEW YORK

A Ballantine Book
Published by The Ballantine Publishing Group
Copyright © 1998 by Scott Gray
This book contains an excerpt from *A Voice and a Dream* by Richard Crouse, published by Ballantine Books.
Copyright © 1998 by Richard Crouse.

Cover photo © Dan Flood/Visages

http://www.randomhouse.com/BB/

Library of Congress Catalog Card Number: 98-93424

ISBN 0-345-42936-2

Manufactured in the United States of America

First Edition: December 1998

10   9   8   7   6   5   4   3   2   1

ON
HER
WAY

By Scott Gray
Published by Ballantine Books:

HEART SONG: *The Story of Jewel*
ON HER WAY: *The Shania Twain Story*

Books published by The Ballantine Publishing Group are available at quantity discounts on bulk purchases for premium, educational, fund-raising, and special sales use. For details, please call 1-800-733-3000.

Contents

Acknowledgments

"A happy heart comes first, then the happy face. I believe in that very much. . . . Just learning that life has to go on and you have to make it go on. . . . That's all there is to it."
—SHANIA TWAIN

It's been said that a close look at the details of a person's life can reveal its passion. That, in a nutshell, was my inspiration in putting together this book: to relate the details of Shania Twain's life in hopes of revealing the passion that drives her.

Those who contributed energy, ideas, and expertise include Heather Poort, Parker Cross, Gene Taback, and the pros at Ballantine Books: Cathy Repetti, Mark Rifkin, Betsy Flagler, Nancy Delia, and Caron Harris.

Thanks Mom and Dad!

ON
HER
WAY

✻ 1 ✻

Get the Party Started

"Shania Twain—there's nobody like her."
—TRISHA YEARWOOD

"There's a tough side of me that comes across in my songs—a side women seem to pick up on. Don't let this frilly look fool you."
—SHANIA

This is it. All the lights go out, and your sense of hearing really perks up. Darkness makes the low rumble of the crowd sound that much deeper, like distant thunder rolling in. You wonder if this is how it felt on Krakatoa just before the volcano blew its top. The pit of your stomach is churning like lava, but its origin is pure emotion. You waited three years for this, and you are far past pumped.

It's a warm June night at the Shoreline Amphitheater in Mountain View, California, about a half hour's drive from San Francisco. This evening it's just you and a few thousand cheering folks who've taken Shania Twain up on her invitation to "come on over." And guess what—she's just as excited to see you as you are to see her. "It's going to be a big party and I'm the hostess," she has said in anticipation of this, her first world tour.

This may be her first full-length tour, but the spotlight has been on Shania nonstop since her breakthrough album, *The Woman in Me,* was released in 1995. More than ten million copies have been sold in the United States alone, making it one of only five albums by a female artist ever to reach that level of domestic success. (Alanis Morissette's *Jagged Little Pill,* Whitney Houston's self-titled debut, Carole King's *Tapestry,* and Mariah Carey's *Music Box* are the others.) Other evidence of the album's unprecedented popularity include:

- It broke the record for most weeks at the top of *Billboard*'s Top Country Albums chart. Shania's twenty-nine weeks surpassed the previous marks held by Wynonna Judd and Mary Chapin Carpenter.

- It broke the record for most weeks in the top ten by a female country artist on *Billboard*'s list of albums for all genres. Shania's twenty-eight weeks exceeded the mark previously held by Reba McEntire.

The Woman in Me was certified four times platinum just ten months after release, the fastest ever by a female country performer. It is by far the biggest-selling album by a woman in country music history, overtaking *Patsy Cline's 12 Greatest Hits* by several million copies in about one-twentieth the time. Shania has earned her spurs, no two ways about it, but she isn't letting success go to her head. "Statistics will deceive you," she told reporter Brian Mansfield. "I'm a long way from being bigger than Patsy Cline."

Maybe so. But a look beyond mere sales numbers reveals that *The Woman in Me* was a wake-up call for folks who thought they knew all about what country music had to offer. The album broke such new ground that few knew what to make of it at first. That was evident in one writer's initial assessment: "*The Woman in Me* feels manufactured, as though it were made by people who've memorized their material without truly understanding it. In other words, the perennial dilemma of all outsiders."

In retrospect, the album was seen, as journalist Bruce Feiler described it, as "the most significant breakthrough in country music in the last decade." Its impact was undeniable: it spawned imitators, inspired established artists, and helped cause a quantum shift in the fan base. "There's a lot of people who listen to my album who listen to the Smashing Pumpkins and there are others who might have a George Strait album along with mine. It's a shame to have your music restricted to any particular audience," Shania explains.

Even "New Traditionalist" George Strait seemed to have discovered *The Woman in Me.* His 1996 CMA (Country Music Association) Album of the Year, *Blue Clear Sky*, sounded distinctly post-Shania, especially on the upbeat title track. In terms of recent Nashville history, it was a case of turnabout being fair play. Strait's back-to-basics ethos had been a huge inspiration to Garth Brooks, the man who poured a shot of arena rock into the New Traditionalist bottle to help create a heady blend called New Country.

Shania followed Garth, spiking that blend with a splash of Country Girl Power. The next thing Music City knew, its music was wearing a bright red dress and dancing on the tables. As she put it in a *Calgary Sun* interview, "We've opened up our own way and I think a lot of people have taken advantage of it and that's great . . ." You might say that if George Strait is the rudder keeping Nashville on course, Shania Twain is the wave carrying it into the future.

> "They were unpredictable. They had a very funky attitude and a sense of humor that I love to play with. And they were a little bit daring, quite daring for country music at the time."
> —SHANIA on the songs from *The Woman in Me*

The Woman in Me gave Music City a friendly smack on the behind and helped prove once and for all that a woman can dictate her own terms, write her own songs, and still make it big in country music. Shania's attitude reflects not a total rejection of the "Stand by Your Man" stance of traditional Nashville, but an updated view that proclaims, in effect, "I'll stand by you if you stand by me. Otherwise, don't let the door hit you on the way out." What's more, Shania broke all the rules about how a nice country girl was supposed to dress and move.

"I know what I want," Shania asserted. "I see no reason why I shouldn't go out and get it. If I use a little sex appeal and I have a little fun, what's wrong with that?" Not a thing; in fact it was exactly what Nashville needed. Songs such as "Any Man of Mine" and "(If You're Not in It for Love) I'm Outta Here" were anthems for a feisty but not divisive style of feminism that struck a chord with both younger and older women. It was a delicate balance, and Shania hit it just right. "I get a lot of letters from women who have teenage daughters; and they have turned their daughter on to my music," Shania told writer Robert K. Oermann.

The success of *The Woman in Me* made Shania one of the prime movers in a shake-up that was long overdue. Country music has long been a man's world, and the women who were in that world had to fight twice as hard every step of the way.

Used to be a gal could hardly get her foot in the door unless she was "the token chick on the label," as Trisha Yearwood put it in *Country Weekly*.

But that worm has started to turn. Since the women had to be absolutely unique in order to stand out, they naturally were making the most personal and creative music around. The result: "Women are leading the pack right now," as Mindy McCready concludes. The guys still out-number the gals by a wide margin on record labels, but women have carved out a bigger niche than ever before.

For example, the top fifteen songs on *Billboard's* 1994 year-end singles chart contained fourteen performed by men and just one by a woman (Tri-sha Yearwood). Same chart and parameters two years later, the ratio was three-to-one, a marked improvement (three of the hits were from *The Woman in Me*). In the same span (1994–96) on the year-end album chart, the ladies went from hav-ing just two of the top fifteen (both by Reba McEntire) to having five (including the number-one spot with *The Woman in Me*).

Those results might not look dramatic, but progress is being made, and the women are coming on strong. Shania gives credit where it's due, telling Tamara Saviano of *Country Weekly*, "It's a compliment if people think I'm a role model for other female artists. But before me, obviously, was Reba, and before Reba, there was Dolly

Parton. I think there always has been, and always will be, women role models."

Again, it's a case of tables turning. There are those who claim that as the men of country have gotten harder to tell apart, the women have grown more distinctive. According to Trisha Yearwood in *Country Weekly*, "Our image choices are endless. It's not that way for the guys." Shania and her sisters—Jo Dee, Faith, Trisha, Mindy, Chely, Deana, Reba, LeAnn, and on down the line—all fashion their own style. It's almost as if the men (with a few exceptions) are restricted to one path. But the gals can mix and match traditional roles with their own creative instincts, rather than follow the herd.

> "One of the virtues of these modern liberated times is that women can, in country music anyway, be sensitive, smart, aggressive and wholesome, all at the same time. You're never sure if you want to buy her a glass of milk or a double bourbon."
> —MARY CHAPIN CARPENTER

Country music's new female artists are a complex breed, more in tune with the full spectrum of music and attitudes than most of the Nashville men, and perhaps better able to filter their sensibilities through their songs. A glance at the lists

of artists' favorite records for 1997, compiled by
Nick Krewen in an article for *Country Weekly*, shows
incredible range: two albums by Prince and one
by Aerosmith on LeAnn Rimes's list; Tracy Chapman, Elton John, and Celine Dion among Michelle
Wright's picks; Shawn Colvin, the Wallflowers,
and Sheryl Crow on Deana Carter's list . . . All of
it mixed in with the Vince Gills and Alan Jacksons
you'd expect to find. The sisters of New Country
are doing it for themselves, and millions of fans
are loving it.

To openhearted country music lovers these
women are a breath of fresh air, but the winds of
change always make the old guard a little snippy.
There are *rules*, you see, and any artist who doesn't
follow them is going to catch hell. Truth be told,
Shania is seen as a threat by certain nostalgic crybabies in the media and jealous types in Music
City who are threatened by the idea of women,
like Shania, who don't fit the myth that beauty,
brains, grit, and talent can't all exist in one person. "I think we've found that inner self-confidence
that lets us be women and be proud of being
women," Mindy McCready asserts.

Shania is brimming with "that inner self-confidence," which sure comes in handy when all
the busybodies start to cackle and crow. When
she chose not to tour right away, some folks
hinted she was a studio creation whose voice
wasn't cut out for the stage. Other people whisper

that her image is too sexy and that she should play down her looks so the critics will respect her. Shania gets called all sorts of things, from fluffy to calculating, but the harsh words are just an indication that she is stirring things up like an artist should.

She lives outside "the weary dance of paired opposites." She is tough to pin down, neither bound by traditional categories nor abandoning them altogether. This is an artist who, when asked by *New Country* magazine to list her five favorite releases of 1995, named albums by the Smashing Pumpkins, Alanis Morissette, Seal, Wynonna, and Wade Hayes. As one *Billboard* reviewer said of Shania's work, "In a very real sense, this is the future of power pop merging with country. In the process, country's traditions are being reinvented and redefined."

In the end, Shania's fans, who listen with their hearts, hold the only opinion that matters, and they give her the freedom to run wild and be creative. And she wants nothing more than to make them happy. "When you're in love with someone, you just want them to love you back," Shania explains. "You want to do everything you can to please them . . . you only hope to get that in return. When fans do that—when they please you because you're pleasing them—it's a great relationship."

The skyrocketing sales of *The Woman in Me* made Shania a superstar, and her follow-up album was one of the most anxiously awaited in recent memory. After hitting the stores in late 1997, *Come on Over* not only shot to the top of the country charts but also came in at number two on *Billboard*'s list for all genres. The international smash "You're Still the One" cracked the top five on both the pop and country charts, and confirmed Shania's appeal with a wide range of listeners. A sold-out world tour cemented her position as the hottest woman in country music.

If all this sounds like a fairy tale, perhaps it is. But keep in mind that Cinderella and Snow White had to suffer and struggle before their dreams came true. Shania is no spoiled little princess; in fact, she worked her tail off to get where she is, singing in bars at the age of eight and working in a Vegas-style revue as a young adult. She's paid her dues and is in no way an overnight sensation. "She's a natural star," comments Susan Ormiston of Canada's W5 TV. "She's not awkward or pretentious. Part of that comes from growing up in difficult circumstances."

Shania's life has gone the route of a country song and a storybook fantasy rolled into one, from her hardscrabble childhood to the tragic loss of her parents in a car wreck to the heights of country music fame and then some. Even the storybook part hasn't been entirely peach pie. Shania has been the focus of debate about her heritage, her position as a role model for young women, and what her crossover success means for country music's future. With regard to the criticism, she has tried to take it in stride for the most part, telling *USA Today*, "I kind of expected it. I guess all newcomers run into that. There's no resentment on my part. The fans dug the album and I'm thrilled to death."

While her public life is hectic, to say the least, Shania is still a hometown girl at heart. In spite of the grueling pace she sets for herself, she keeps her sense of balance—thanks in large part to her producer/songwriter husband, "Mutt" Lange. He is the cherry in Shania's fruit cocktail, and their marriage has turned out to be one of the sweetest unions in the history of music. Mutt wrote or cowrote nearly every song on *The Woman in Me* and *Come on Over*, and he produced both albums as well. Shania wrote the romantic "You're Still the One" in Mutt's honor, and it proved to be one of the biggest crossover hits of the decade.

From start to finish Shania's story is a rags-to-riches yarn, the stuff Nashville legends are made of, tracing a route from northern Canada down to Music City, U.S.A., with plenty of detours and colorful characters along the way. As a *People* magazine writer put it, Shania "holds bragging rights to the toughest tale."

That's half the picture, but the best part is how that "toughest tale" has shaped her into such a hopeful, inspired person. As she once wrote in the

Canadian magazine *Country*: "Through it all, I still believe that love and happiness are the most important things and to never lose sight of them. Life passes us by very quickly whether we are happy or unhappy. So, I put most of my energy into happiness. You can't have a happy face if you don't have a happy heart."

❊ 2 ❊

Make the Music Go Bang

"Perhaps rock's influence on Ms. Twain is not so much musical as it is philosophical. Rock's iconoclasm has freed her from country's traditions and allowed her to create a country music that is hers alone."
—NATASHA STOVAL, *The New York Times*

No doubt about it, Shania Twain is the most innovative artist in country music today. Her songs, her style, and her success testify to her possession of the desire and the talent to take the genre to places it has never been. She's truly living up to her adopted first name, an Ojibwa Indian word that means "I'm on my way." Some might say she has already arrived, but the creative strides Shania is making are proof that she is just getting started.

It's no surprise that in the process she has made some folks in Nashville a little antsy. But the good news is that Shania is staying true to her fans, her craft, and herself. If that means working outside of the status quo, so be it. After all, Shania has been crossing borders all her life, and she isn't about to stop being her own woman or making music her own way. Shania trusts that her fans "get it," and they've justified her faith with their support. As she said in a *Country Weekly* article by Tamara Saviano, "I think fans are totally unlimited. Their minds are completely open. They're always interested in what's creative and new and refreshing."

It's been a decade or so since Dwight Yoakam—country's resident creative genius—swept away what was left of Nashville's artistic limits with a hybrid of roots-revival country and a kitchen sink full of sixties radio pop, postpunk indie rock, jazz, R&B, you name it. Dwight was the prime mover in waking folks up to the legacy of Buck Owens, the fellow who played a huge part in the shaping of modern country, and whose importance we'll look at in depth.

It's also been about a decade since Garth Brooks blew the gates off of Music City's commercial barriers. Before Garth it was fairly uncommon for a country record to sell more than a million copies. His watershed release, *No Fences*, went thirteen times platinum in the U.S. Shania is the one country star who's come close to reaching those numbers, but she was quick to acknowledge in an interview with Ken Churilla in the October 1996 *Country Song Roundup*, "I don't think it's realistic for me or anyone else to ever expect to sell what Garth sells."

What she has done is take the creative options and crossover aesthetic of Dwight and Garth and tweak them to the limit. With help from her husband, Mutt, the brilliant songwriter and producer behind some of the best-selling rock albums ever, Shania built on the foundation that Dwight and Garth laid. She added her own attitudes and sensibilities and came up with *The Woman in Me.* James Hunter put it well when he wrote of "Twain's underlying message that an ordinary person with artistry and a touch or two of star quality could make the kind of genuine although not roots-obsessed music for which Brooks paved the way."

While you can't talk about New Country without mentioning Garth, his is, for an obvious reason, a primarily male perspective (albeit an enlightened one); his best work evokes echoes of Merle Haggard and the Rolling Stones. Shania, in contrast, tells the women's side of things. (Garth could no more have done "Any Man of Mine" than Shania could pull off "The Rodeo.") She has forebears related to Garth's but a bit more eclectic, more like Dwight's: i.e., the Beatles and Buck Owens. A case can be made that New Country owes as much to Bakersfield—home to Merle and

Buck—and Britain—home to the Beatles and the Stones—as it owes to Nashville.

It's fitting that when Shania was born—in the summer of '65—popular music (both rock and country) crackled with new freedom and cross-over energy. The British Invasion bands were, among other things, turning the masses on to the sounds of neglected rhythm-and-blues artists such as Chuck Berry. The Beatles were the single greatest influence on current popular music (including country, for better or worse), and one reason was their willingness to blur boundaries, borrow from unrelated sources, and create new musical hybrids.

It's no shock Shania dreams of a Beatles reunion in her hit song "When." She loves to attract new fans by spicing her songs with the flavors of other genres. The Beatles set the standard for doing this, drawing from any and every source that suited their artistic vision. That's one of the reasons why they are the most influential group ever: they revered all music but were slaves to none.

Of course, the Fab Four was influenced by American rhythm and blues, citing Chuck Berry as a prime inspiration. John Lennon once said, "If you were going to give rock 'n' roll another name, you might call it 'Chuck Berry.' " But the Beatles also harbored a deep admiration for American country and western; their 1965 UK album *Help!* included a goofy but good-faith version of "Act

Naturally," sung complete with English accent. The song had been a number-one hit for Buck Owens two years earlier. (Buck and Ringo cut a duet of the song in 1989.)

The crossover winds blew on both sides of the Atlantic that year—and on both sides of the fences that were supposed to separate rock from country. Buck had again topped the C&W charts, this time with "I've Got a Tiger by the Tail," the title track from his new album. He took out an ad in *Music City News* that proclaimed, "I Shall Make No Record That Is Not a Country Record," but with its electric guitars and 4/4 backbeat, *Tiger* made more than a passing nod to rock and roll. It was downright flirtatious.

Tiger included a version of "Memphis," a song by the same Chuck Berry whose name was synonymous with rock and roll itself. Buck said the song was rockabilly—to his reasoning a form of country. That's true enough in part, to the same extent that a dish of fudge ripple ice cream is a form of vanilla; in rockabilly, the chocolate half is that ol' devil rock and roll.

So it was 1965 and the world's biggest pop-rock act was exploring country while the top C&W artist dabbled in rock. What was the upshot of all this crossing over (and what's all this got to do with Shania)? In essence, the fields where New Country later sprang up were being plowed by Buck Owens and the Beatles the year Shania was born.

If that seems off-the-wall, think of it this way: New Country arose from a spirit as old as time itself: the spirit of freedom. It was no accident that Garth titled his milestone album *No Fences*. Shania is like-minded; she considered *No Inhibitions* as the title for her third album before opting for *Come on Over*. By stretching country music's limits, Dwight, Garth, Shania, and company are pushing the integration of Anglo-Celtic and African forms, a process that's been going on for a long time.

Hank Williams, the father of modern country, learned how to play guitar from a black bluesman known as Tee Tot. Jimmie Rodgers, "the man who started it all" (according to his plaque at the Country Music Hall of Fame), leaned toward the unfortunately named "nigger blues," as producer Ralph Peer was quoted as saying by writer Nolan Porterfield in his book *Jimmie Rodgers: The Life and Times of America's Blue Yodeler*. Rodgers even tried out for a spot in a Louis Armstrong jazz combo in the late 1920s. (How's that for crossover!)

Folks love to talk about what is and isn't "authentic" country, as if the definition is static. But a person who's afraid Shania is taking the music too far from its roots is forgetting that country has never been "pure," and that the artists we peg as "pure and authentic" weren't bound by such labels until their careers were over. Read the following excerpt on Emmett Miller—who, according to the *Country Music Encyclopedia*, had an "impact on such seminal figures as Jimmie Rodgers, Bob Wills, and Hank Williams"—and think of it when you talk about who and what is "real" country: "He fit none of our neat categories: he wasn't exactly blues, not quite country, not entirely pop, more than comedy" (Charles Wolfe, in the liner notes to *The Minstrel Man from Georgia—Emmett Miller*).

Now, the branch that connects Shania Twain to Emmett Miller on the tree of music may take a stretch to reach. Then again the roots rarely look like the fruits; and besides, the link here is one of spirit, not sound. The word "crossover" isn't used as a compliment these days, but it does represent the dynamic that keeps country music "creative and new and refreshing," as Shania put it.

It's a spirit that comes from seeing all sides of life (and music) and learning to love the whole ball of wax. Shania was born into an era of constant change in a complex world, so she knows how to adjust and adapt but still be true to herself. She's both fun loving and serious, private and public, artistic and practical. In short she is an honest-to-goodness, complicated, and fascinating person, an ideal ambassador for country music.

⇸ 3 ⇷

Hit the Ground Running

"I never wanted to be the star—I just wanted to be Stevie Wonder's backup singer."
—SHANIA

Of course it wasn't just the music world that tumbled in waves of change during the summer of 1965. America had escalated its role in Vietnam, black leader Malcolm X had been assassinated, and in August there were deadly riots in the Watts section of Los Angeles. A book called *The Feminine Mystique* had fired up the women's movement. The modern world was in the throes of change.

That same tumultuous summer, on the Canadian side of the Detroit River, another kind of change was taking place. Little did expectant parents Sharon and Clarence Edwards, and their daughter, Jill, know that years later their newest addition—from head to toe a citizen of the modern world—would rock country music into the twenty-first century. As an adult, Shania would later profess, "Well, we're in a time where, I mean, you can pretty much do anything creatively now. You can wear anything, you can say anything, you can pretty much do anything and get away with it, you know?"

It was on August 28, 1965, in the city of Windsor, Ontario, that a beautiful baby girl named Eileen Regina Edwards was born. What's that? You've never heard the name Eileen Regina Edwards? Well, a lot has happened in her life since then, and she is now known to millions of fans as the incredible singer/songwriter Shania Twain. With a pair of multiplatinum albums under her belt, plus a self-titled debut that has turned gold, that baby girl has grown into an amazing woman standing high atop the country music mountain.

In the decades that followed her entry into this world, she's gone through a couple of rebirths and more than her share of change. In fact, the tracks of this Twain's life have taken more twists than a rattlesnake on hot sand—and the first big bend came before she was old enough to grasp the implications. Even as she was learning to walk and talk, her parents were growing apart, and shortly after the arrival of their third daughter, Carrie-Ann, they gave up on their marriage for keeps. Although they didn't legally divorce until several years later, there was nothing to keep Sharon in Windsor, so she took her three girls and headed north toward a new start.

It might be said that Shania was reborn for the first time in the wake of her mom and dad's parting. Windsor, the place of her birth, was to become merely the name of a distant city. Clarence would go his own way, never again to play a parental role in Shania's life. By the time she'd grown up enough to have known her blood father or her birthplace, both were in the distant past.

As you might imagine, this was a tough time for Sharon and her daughters. They had no easy road in front of them and nowhere to call home. Money was tight, the girls had no father, and Sharon was facing the future all alone. After a period of looking around for the right place to put down new roots, the foursome settled in Timmins, Ontario, a city of about 48,000 located roughly four hundred miles equidistant from Ottawa (the national capital) and Toronto (the provincial capital). "As far as square mileage, it's probably one of the largest cities in the world. But it's a lot of property and a lot of moose, not a lot of people," explains Shania.

The local economy is built on forestry and mining. The nearby Kidd Creek Mine is one of the largest sources of zinc in the world; a fifteen-ton boulder containing zinc-bearing ore sits outside the chamber-of-commerce building on McIntyre Road. The thirty-five townships within the city boundaries constitute more land area than the entire state of Rhode Island, and there are hundreds of lakes and streams within that land area. Winters are long, with nighttime temperatures staying well below freezing into early May. Timmins bills itself as "the gateway to the Northeastern Arctic and Greenland," so you know it's colder than a snow dog's nose. Snowshoes and snowmobiles are de rigueur for much of the year. Timmins boasts all the amenities of any other North American city its size, but the geography and weather make for hearty and rugged folks.

It was here that Sharon fell in love with the man Shania came to know as her father: Gerald Twain, a full-blood Ojibwa Indian. A wise person who understood the value of family, he was quick to accept Jill, Eileen (Shania), and Carrie-Ann as his own daughters. Soon after Sharon's first marriage was legally ended, Jerry and Sharon were joined in wedlock, and the girls were legally adopted by Jerry.

This meant that Shania and her sisters were to be, from that time forward, full-fledged members of the Temagami Anishnawbe Bear Island First Nation. Later on Sharon and Jerry added a pair of boys, Mark and Darryl, to the Twain clan. The family was close-knit, and there was never a doubt that all the kids were equal in the eyes of their parents, their tribe, or each other. The terms "step" and "half," as in stepfather or half brother, were strictly forbidden at the Twains' house. "We were all just family," Shania told Barbara Hager.

The cultural history of the Ojibwa Indians is intricate and rich, yet their name is unfamiliar to the majority of North Americans. In the 1800s the Ojibwa, who lived along the shores of the upper Great Lakes, drove the Sioux down the Mississippi in conflicts over wild rice–growing lands. Some of the Ojibwa ventured west to the plains, while others remained in the woodlands of Michigan and Ontario. Taken together the various Ojibwa tribes now compose one of the five largest Indian populations north of Mexico.

Ojibwa culture has left its impression on mainstream North American art. Longfellow's famous poem *The Song of Hiawatha* draws heavily on Ojibwa stories (although the name Hiawatha derives from Iroquois sources). Music fans who recall Ontario native Gordon Lightfoot's folk-rock epic "Wreck of the Edmond Fitzgerald," with its reference to the Chippewa legends of Lake Superior, may be interested to learn that the Chippewa are a cultural-regional subgroup of the Woodlands Ojibwa. Shania's fame brought renewed attention to the Ojibwa in both Canada and the United States, and she is quite proud of that fact.

As the legally adopted children of Jerry Twain, Shania and her sisters are accorded official First Nations status; they are registered as 50 percent North American Indian and are considered as such regardless of genealogy (their birth parents were of French and Irish descent). The girls were raised under the strong, positive influence of Jerry Twain and his family. Shania recalls that Grandpa Jerry and Grandma Selina, Jerry's parents, "loved us as though we were their very own grandchildren ... and we were equally accepted by his other relatives."

The entire extended family took part in the lives of Jill, Shania, Carrie-Ann, Mark, and Darryl. Summer weekends were spent on the Matagami Reserve, playing with cousins. Shania's grandpa spoke the Ojibwa language and taught Shania how to track rabbits. Her grandmother sewed clothes for her and told her stories. "Being raised by a full-blooded Indian and being part of his family and their culture from a young age is all I've ever known. That heritage is my heart and my soul, and I'm very proud of it," Shania affirms.

In most respects Shania was like any other young child. She laughed and played, was fascinated by animals and nature, and stayed blissfully unaware of adult worries—at least early on. But there was a special quality that set her apart from other kids: she sang like a little angel. Her love of music was evident right from the start; it was as if she'd been born with a song in her soul. For instance, not only did she sing "Twinkle, Twinkle, Little Star," with the skill of a much older child, she was also inclined to toy with phrasing and tone.

She began playing with melody at a very young age—making up new parts to the songs she heard on her mom and dad's eight-track player—and her parents took notice. As she told *Interview* magazine, "I guess when you hear a six-year-old child harmonizing, you start to pay attention." Shania was naturally shy, and singing was simply a way she liked to play. "I would just sit for a long time by myself and do nothing else but sing," she recalls. Her mom and dad decided that if one of their offspring had talent, it wasn't to be wasted. Anxious to see if other people heard what she and Jerry heard, Sharon sometimes lifted Shania onto the counter at local diners and coaxed her into singing for the patrons.

Another of Shania's first stabs at singing in public came during show-and-tell period in the first grade. She chose to show her special talent by singing a John Denver song, "Take Me Home, Country Roads." The year was 1970, and Denver

was to become one of the most popular artists of
the decade, but his music just wasn't deemed
cool by that roomful of Timmins first-graders.
Shania had no way to predict how her pint-
size peers would react, and nothing could have
prepared her for the harsh reception she got.
Shania sang her heart out—it was a tune she
truly loved—but the reward turned out to be a
dose of teasing by all the little brats who didn't
know any better.

To top off their taunting, they branded her
with a nickname: "Twang." For a modern country
musician to be known as Twang would be an
honor; it has been said that the word is to country
music as "soul" is to rhythm and blues. If you
consider all that Shania has done in and for
country music since then, the put-down oozes
irony. Still the teasing would have hurt a whole
lot less if she'd known then what she knows now.
Call her Twang these days and Shania will probably say, "Thank you!"

Yet the sensitive six-year-old that Shania was
back then came away from that day with a suspicion that "country music wasn't really the thing
to sing." Trivial though it may seem today, the
moment helped set the course of Shania's life and
career. Her natural inclination was to question
herself more than she did the whelps who made
fun of her. The desire to be adored, the fear of
being judged—these are issues that can create in-

ternal conflict in performers of any age. And in the same way that intense pressure forms precious jewels in nature, it shapes artists in unusual and beautiful ways.

Shania told about the incident in a letter she wrote to her fans back in 1994, printed by the Canadian music magazine *Country.* "All my class-mates thought I was being a 'show off' and it really created serious inhibitions for me," she re-called. "From that point on, I was afraid to per-form." It might be hard to reconcile images of the confident woman Shania is today with the por-trait of a scared little girl she paints in her letter. But the sting of that first-grade memory lingered and may have had a couple of long-term effects: first as a motivation for her always to work extra hard to justify audience approval, and second in driving her search for varied styles to weave into her music.

The rebuke of her grade-school mates made Shania wary of "showing off" her gift in public. Had it not been for the prodding of Sharon and Jerry, young Shania might have channeled her talent into a private hobby rather than inter-national superstardom. "I didn't want to take it that seriously. I enjoyed being creative and do-ing it for myself," Shania told reporter Howard Cohen. "It's like someone saying, 'You sound great in the shower, you mind if we bring an audience tomorrow?'"

As an adult, she concedes that there was an upside to what her parents did. "My parents forced me to perform, which in the long run was the best thing because I was [by nature] quite a recluse," she explained in *Cash Box*. "If not for my parents I'd still be singing in my bedroom . . ." (Shania has since noted that perhaps "forced" was not the best choice of words.) It's possible that Nashville would never have heard of Shania had she been left to her own devices.

Sharon in particular had no intention of letting that happen. She believed her second daughter was a prodigy, and she set up gigs for Shania in every venue she could find, from community centers and local fairs to family gatherings. One of Shania's more memorable shows was at a home for the elderly where her great-grandfather lived. The seniors had tricky standards. "I'd have some people going 'I can't hear anything—is she playing anything?' and others complaining that it was too loud," Shania told Anthony Noguera of *FHM* magazine.

It's natural to assume that Sharon had mixed motives for wanting her child to be a star, but Shania insists that her mom's desires had little to do with "bragging rights." Sharon was desperate to see her progeny escape poverty, so she did all she could to give Shania a head start on the road to financial independence. It was the age-old desire to see your children have a better life than your own that fueled Sharon's drive.

Shania's father also offered more than passive support; he introduced her to the magic of guitars. Jerry was a self-taught amateur with a pretty good ear and enough skill to cover his favorite songs on the acoustic. Jill had been given a classical guitar, but it was Shania who always seemed to be holding it, and since she was already a singer, it was only natural that she learn to play.

It was Jerry who gave Shania her first lessons in frets and chords and tuning. She picked up the basics at an age when the guitar was longer than she was tall and her arms barely fit around its wooden body. Shania didn't go on to become a master of the craft, but not being a virtuoso is no problem. She uses her guitar as a songwriting tool, and to that end it serves her well. "I love to write stories," she has professed. "I like to give every song its own personality and attitude and to sing each one in its own style." Again, looking back, Shania recalls the mixed feelings that went with loving music and being asked to perform in public. "I would play 'til my fingers were bruised, and I loved it! But I never enjoyed the pressure of being a performer."

With Dad tutoring her on guitar and Mom setting up gigs, Shania was gearing up to take the local music scene by the horns. Sadly, her childhood was being at least partly trampled under the hooves. "I dreamed about being a kid," she confided in a *People* magazine article. Only eight years old, Shania was being steered toward a life in show business. The self-described "little country girl with this huge guitar" was fed onstage patter by her mother and father in an attempt to give her more "stage presence."

She was plenty aware of the family hopes that had been put on her small shoulders. At each juncture of Shania's budding career, the Twains sacrificed so that she'd have access to microphones and stage clothes and sheet music. "My mother did it all. She got me all those things. I still don't know how she did it, but she did," Shania marvels in retrospect. Sharon even drove the young performer to Toronto for voice lessons when time and money allowed. Shania felt the caring and support, but she also sensed the pressure that goes with carrying other people's dreams. The whole family was caught up in the notion that one of their own might be the next Loretta Lynn.

It wasn't always easy to find venues for a pre-teen singer in Timmins, but that didn't deter Sharon. She worked nights in the kitchen at the Mattagami Hotel, and she arranged for Shania to sing and play there in the wee hours after liquor was no longer being served. "I used to be dragged out of bed at 1:00 in the morning and they'd bring me to the local club to play with the band," Shania explains.

With her mom and dad leading her to the stage, Shania felt the eyes of the curious afterhours patrons focus on her. The house band may have been amused, but they didn't let it show too much. "I wish they would have made those half-width size guitars when I was eight," Shania jokes when recalling those nights. But when she sang, people tended to forget that she was just a kid. A wellspring of intensity bubbled up from inside her; she sang adult songs in an adult way.

It must have been a strange scene: this little girl with a big guitar, singing her heart out for a small crowd of loggers and miners, past the hour when most kids are snuggled warmly in bed and dreaming. While she recalls that the adventure and attention were fun, Shania also admits to having felt out of place. "It's awkward to be in a bar when everyone's drunk and smoking, but I had to do it anyway," she said in *Maclean's*. Yet today Shania looks back with pride and a sense of wonder at how brave she was back then. She also asserts that Jerry and Sharon were supportive and caring parents. "My parents were loving," she states without reservation.

Shania also insists that her act was no joke, no mere novelty. She took her "job" very seriously.

Shania told journalist Howard Cohen that her parents had explained, "You're in an adult world; you can't be a crybaby." She took those words to heart, and when she was nervous they gave her the power to choke back her fears and get to the task at hand. That may seem like a crazy thing for a nine-year-old to need to do, but as her folks said, she was in an adult world.

Jerry and Sharon shared a passion for what was then still known as country and western music. They listened to their favorite artists just about every day on the eight-track player in the house and the radio in their truck. The 1970s were a very intriguing and important time in the history of the genre. This was also a formative period for Shania, a time when she was tuned in to many of the artists who are now seen as her most direct influences. A look at what was going on in Nashville back then sheds some light on the music Shania is making today.

During the mid-seventies country music was split roughly into two camps: the outlaws and country-pop. Sharon and Jerry Twain listened to the best of both styles, and Shania heard it all during her preteen and teenage years. The legacy of country-pop and the outlaws can be detected on *The Woman in Me*, although Shania is so unique that it is impossible to trace her roots directly to one artist or period. In terms of sound and presentation, *The Woman in Me* has more in common with country-pop than the outlaws. At the same time, you could infer that Shania learned a thing or two about attitude from the outlaws.

Billy Joe Shaver, Willie Nelson, Waylon Jennings, Kris Kristofferson, Tompall Glaser, and David Allen Coe are all identified with the so-called outlaw movement. Like all movements in popular music, it was largely about fashion and marketing: long hair, denim and leather, and beards, sixties urban counterculture infiltrates stuffy old Nashville, and all that sort of thing. It certainly worked; the first country album to sell a million copies was the compilation record *Wanted! The Outlaws!* in 1976. (A year later Waylon got busted for cocaine possession, recorded "Don't You Think This Outlaw Bit Done Got Out of Hand?" and effectively put an end to the trend.)

Shania and the women of New Country have much in common with the outlaws: a style and attitude that makes the conservatives nervous, a willingness to sing about subjects that were once taboo, a knack for blending other genres with country, and huge commercial success. The outlaws helped jar Nashville out of the dull funk it was mired in prior to their arrival. They cribbed liberally from Chuck Berry and dared to stay independent the way Buck Owens had done a decade earlier. With their posthippie roughneck image and refusal to do things Music Row's way, they stood in direct contrast to the other prominent style of the era: country-pop, especially as put together by producer Billy Sherrill.

Sherrill, too, injected a dose of rock into country, but it was less blues-based and more classical. He was influenced by Phil Spector, the man who some credit with inventing grand pop production. (You can hear Phil's work on the next-to-last Beatles record, *Let It Be*.) Billy Sherrill applied Spector's "wall of sound" techniques—using strings and vocal choruses and such for a layered effect—to create a pop brand of country that proved to be very popular.

A lot of folks sure have short memories and/or a knack for revising history, especially the people who claim Shania Twain is violating Nashville's hallowed canons. The reality is that each new wave of artists comes along and makes a unique brand of country. At the time the new style seems a radical break from tradition, and the old guard gets riled up about it. But if the new songs are worth a hoot, the new artists bump the older artists off the charts. After a while the new style becomes passé and the old new artists turn into the new old guard. When the next generation rides into town, the whole thing begins all over again. It's a healthy cycle, it keeps things in balance. The old-timers stop the youngsters from straying too far from tradition, and the new artists bring fresh blood into the music.

In a sense the same cycle was at work in the Twains' house. Sharon and Jerry saw to it that Shania's repertoire was country all the way. In doing so, they set her little feet square in a solid country base. As she got older the rock and pop influences seeped in, but it was never in doubt that Shania would always be country first. She sang classics such as "Kaw-Liga," a Hank Williams original that Charley Pride had taken to number three in '69. She sang "Delta Dawn," the tune Tanya Tucker took to number six on the country charts in '72 and that Helen Reddy took to number one on the pop charts the following year. She also did a couple of Dolly Parton tunes, including "Coat of Many Colors," perhaps the one song on Shania's set list that, more than any other, hit home.

Dolly had been one of twelve children growing up in poverty on a family farm in tiny Locust Ridge, Tennessee. One fall when she was eight years old her mom stitched together a coat out of quilting scraps for Dolly to wear to school. "It hurt me so bad when the kids laughed, because I was so proud of it," Dolly has often recalled. "I especially liked the bright colors, and I thought I was the prettiest thing in school." It's a country classic, with lyrics that are both honest and nostalgic, sweet and sad. Shania felt the truth of

Dolly's signature song in her bones. "I could relate to hardship, the tensions that can be in a household when there's not enough money to go grocery shopping," she once told interviewer Richard Cromelin. "You grow up fast in an environment that's a little underprivileged."

More than any other woman in country music, Dolly Parton was Shania's childhood heroine. Years later, on an airline flight to Nashville, Shania encountered Dolly for the first time. Shania was humming one of her own songs to herself, and Dolly asked what it was, but a starstruck Shania was too shy to answer. "My one chance to talk to Dolly Parton and I didn't take it!" she recalls with regret.

The two women have a lot in common. Dolly is strong-willed, talented, and smart. At the peak of her career she was an international star, crossing over onto the pop charts and enjoying huge commercial success. She was misunderstood by folks who couldn't see past her sexy image, and she was often criticized for breaking with Nashville tradition, but she was instrumental in exposing a mass audience to country music. "Dolly has done everything. She's an exceptional writer. She's an actress. She's a great personality. She's everything," Shania exclaims.

Like her idol, Shania was born with a wooden spoon in her mouth. Her family was dirt-poor, a fact that grew more and more acute to Shania as the soft focus of early childhood wore off. In the Twain household there were rarely extra portions at the dinner table. "If you decided to take an extra potato, someone didn't get a potato at all," she once told Johanna Schneller in *Chatelaine* magazine. Shania also recalls feeling ill at ease about having cookies at a friend's house, knowing her parents would be hard-pressed to return the favor. Once, when a young friend did come over, Shania gasped with surprise when the friend took more than her share of milk.

When a family is as poor as the Twains were, the hope of alleviating their situation can be an overriding drive. The idea that Shania might one day be rich and famous eased the family's emotional burden, but it also guaranteed that she wouldn't complain or refuse when her parents wanted her to get up and sing in the middle of the night. She felt that she had to do it for the good of her parents and siblings, and in a real sense she was right.

This part of Shania's childhood brings up complex social issues. It can be disturbing to see footage of child beauty pageants, or to hear stories about toddlers hitting tennis balls for hours at a time, or to read tell-all bios of the troubled lives of former child actors. The goals of parents, not to mention the lure of financial gain, may lead to decisions that aren't totally in the child's best interest. Few would argue against the idea that a child should be treated like a sentient person, not just a bundle of talents or an object for sale.

But the line between exploitation and encouragement is open to interpretation. "Coming from a poor family, the only thing that's going to get your children anywhere is to just push like hell. And that's what my mother did," Shania told Nicholas Jennings in *Maclean's* magazine. Shania doesn't look back on Jerry and Sharon with any hard feelings; quite the opposite, in fact. She considers the prodding her parents gave to be a crucial part of putting her on the path to a fulfilling life and career.

It turns out that being urged to perform in public, when her gut instinct was to hide, helped restore the confidence she had lost after the show-and-tell incident. Her voice and stage presence, not to mention her business acumen, were already taking shape. At one point, when she was in fifth grade, Shania was asked by her school principal to sing at an afterschool event. The precocious ten-year-old said okay, then went on to list the monitors, mikes, etc. that she would need. She suggested that the principal phone Sharon to schedule the performance. Is it any surprise that Shania is a strong-willed woman who calls her own shots? Taking on grown-up tasks at a young age built up much of the inner strength and self-esteem that serves her so well as an adult.

That particular school gig never actually came to pass, but Shania had bigger fish to fry. While still a child she made it onstage as the opening act for shows featuring national stars such as Gary Buck, one of the most popular and respected of Canada's country musicians. She opened for Anita Perras "when I was just a kid and she was a teenager," as Shania put it. She also appeared with Ronnie Prophet, who had a TV show on the Canadian Broadcasting Company network in the 1970s. Carrol Baker is another whose stage Shania once shared. Baker has been hailed as Canada's first queen of country; she had fourteen straight number-one hits in Canada during one stretch of her CCMA Hall of Honour career.

Shania was growing up fast both as a performer and as a person. By the time she was in her early teens she had paid more dues than some people pay in a lifetime. The dark clouds of her mom's bouts with depression forced Shania to mature quickly. "I ironed Dad's clothes and made porridge in the morning for the kids," she recalled in *People.* Poverty, too, remained an ever-present problem. "We would go for days with just bread and milk and sugar—heat it up in a pot," Shania confessed in *Homemaker's.* "I used to take mustard sandwiches to school, just to have something," she further revealed. "I'd judge other kids' wealth by their lunches. If a kid had baked goods, that was like, oh, they must be rich."

It was a sad state of affairs, and it made Sharon's blue moods even deeper. "We were extremely poor," Shania told *Cash Box*, "and my mother was often depressed with five children and no food to feed them." Shania has often spoken of the emotional effects of not having plenty to eat, how she would tell her teachers that she just didn't feel like eating lunch when the truth was more a case of not having the option. She lied to them out of fear that someone would try to split apart the family.

In his book *Three Chords and the Truth*, Laurence Leamer saw fit to challenge Shania's depiction of the Twain family's circumstances. "Canadians have built their social safety net further off the floor than their neighbors immediately to the south," he wrote, "and few working families exist on diets primarily of potatoes and bread." Leamer went on to contend, "Poverty, however, is a matter of perception. It may well be that this little girl *felt* her poverty the way few others did in school."

Leamer goes on to indict people who "exaggerated their humble origins, believing it made their own successes seem even greater, while in fact it diminished the struggles of their forebears . . ."

In other words, Shania is making her past seem harder than it really was, and thus is doing a dishonor to her parents. Referring directly to such hurtful insinuations, Shania told Brian D. Johnson in *Maclean's*, "I'm not sugarcoating, but I've revealed very little of the true hardship and intensity of my life, and that's the way I'm going to keep it."

Even if you accept the iffy premise that Leamer has access to facts that contradict Shania's version of her own childhood, it's hard to see what purpose is served by nitpicking about the contents of a little girl's stomach. The analysis that she simply "felt her poverty the way few others did" indicates such an inflated sense of omniscience that it's downright funny. He can speculate all he wants on what young Shania may have felt, but he doesn't actually *know* anything about it. He sure wasn't living at the Twains' house, and Shania never said that the family ate nothing but bread and potatoes every day of their lives.

Actually she has often said of the family situation, "I never considered it that bad." At one point Leamer notes that the Twain children were always sent to school in clean, mended clothes. But he doesn't quote Shania on the subject, writing in his own voice as if setting the record straight, when in fact Shania once told Johanna Schneller of *Chatelaine* magazine, "I recognized as a kid that I wasn't the worst off. My mother had a lot of pride. We never went to school dirty or in ripped clothes."

There is little argument about whether Canada has treated its Indians better than the U.S. has treated its own, but that doesn't make it unthinkable that a proud, blue-collar family of seven couldn't have on occasion found itself scraping by on the bare minimum. The press may have picked up on the poverty theme and given it mythical weight, but that says more about the media than it does about Shania. Whatever the state of the Twains' pantry in the 1970s, if Shania's personal accounts of her childhood are taken at face value, they form an image that focuses more on good times than on tough times.

❧ 4 ❧

Bush Life and Stage Lights

"I'm an old-fashioned person and I think country
music helps me stay true to that."
— SHANIA

Shania started writing her own songs before
she'd entered her teens, and these early ditties
show a startling grasp of adult themes. In an article written by Alison Powell for *Interview* magazine, Shania recalled that "people would just shake
their heads" at the thought of such a young girl
putting such detail and emotion into her fictional
tales of woe and heartbreak. She didn't keep a
diary, but her songwriting book served the same
purpose. "I liked to escape my personal life through
my music," she explains.

While she was learning valuable lessons about
how to be confident in public, Shania held on
tight to the private side of herself. She has always
been drawn to secret places where she can be

45

alone with her thoughts. "My mother used to try so hard to catch me songwriting and I would just get so mad at her," she recalled in a *Rolling Stone* article. Shania often sought out the solitude of the forests near her house, where she would build a fire, play her guitar, and let her vivid imagination run free. "If I would hear anyone coming, or calling my name, I would be still or quiet as a mouse until they went away," she confided in her 1994 "fan letter."

She still feels that way about the bush and the isolation it offers her. "I like being secluded. I like solitude. I never want to let go of it. It's a craving for me. I have to be in the bush," Shania explained to Catherine Dunphy of *The Toronto Star*. She once was quoted in *Country America* as saying, "I like chopping wood. I like making fires. I love smelling like fire. That's my favorite smell. I love it when my hair smells like fire."

Her passion for the woods can be traced back to Jerry's influence. He taught his children all the skills of wilderness survival. The Twain family went camping on a regular basis; not to prefab spots where people pitch tents next to garbage cans and cinderblock outhouses, but deep in the heart of the bush. They would sleep under the stars and marvel at the vastness of the night sky, far from the dimming effects of city lights.

Out in the forest Jerry Twain made sure his kids understood that when all the trivia was stripped away, family was what mattered. Jerry also helped foster Shania's love of the Ojibwa heritage that had been given to her. He told her stories and answered her questions about life and nature. He showed her all the types of plants and trees and animals, and he pointed out the star clusters.

Those outings made the bonds of family airtight, and went a long way toward developing Shania's spirituality, but Jerry also gave his kids practical advice about how to survive in the great outdoors. He taught them how to hunt and lay traps and dress wild game. Shania's job was to set snares for the rabbits. "It looks like a guitar string that you rig up in a loop. When the rabbit gives a little tug, it's strangled," Shania revealed in Vancouver's *Province* newspaper. That might sound cruel and unnecessary to city folks, but for the Twains it was neither. On the contrary the experience revealed to Shania the value of all life. Jerry insisted that they eat every animal they killed— not that they could have afforded to waste food. When money was tight, as it usually was, the meat from rabbits and partridge and such was a crucial source of nutrition.

These days she can have anything her stomach asks for, but Shania has chosen to be a vegetarian. It's a decision she made several years ago, one she has never regretted, but she isn't militant about it; she gladly fixes meat dishes for visitors to her table. Shania is a fine cook. She gathered a treasure trove of kitchen wisdom from her mother and grandmother, and she takes great pleasure in making meals for Mutt and herself. "I love to cook. I like to get up in the morning and put a stew on or put soup on," she told Jill Phillips in *Countrybeat* magazine. Shania is careful to never make too much for one meal, as she can't stand to waste food.

Adversity builds character, they say, and Shania is living proof. Being poor was a fact of her early life, but so was having a strong sense of right and wrong. Loyal to her family above all else, she was more concerned with doing her part to help than with fretting over what she might be missing. Whether it was getting her brothers and sisters fed and dressed for school in the morning or doing all of the household chores after school, she kept her priorities straight and didn't slack off.

All the while Sharon tried to nurture her daughter's budding music career. She wanted so badly for Shania to become a star, and she kept up the pressure despite the day-to-day struggles that arose. It was a tenacity and focus she passed along to her daughter. "My mother lived for my career," Shania said. "She knew I was talented and she lived with the hope that my abilities were my chance to do something special." It's been said that you've got to want it to win it, and Sharon definitely wanted it.

Once, when Shania was about twelve, Sharon set up a gig for her in Sudbury as the opener for Canadian singer Mary Bailey, who'd scored a national hit with the song "Mystery Lady." The redheaded Mary had worked the Canadian circuit for years and was well-known in her home country. She had been the opening act on bills for famous American acts, and RCA had released a couple of her singles.

By the time she met Sharon and Shania that night in 1978, Mary was thinking of giving up the spotlight for good. The era was a tough one for Canadian country singers, who were either ignored or treated like second-string artists in relation to their Nashville peers. It was clear to Mary that she was never going to break out as a major figure in country music, at least not on the stage. However, her passion for music still burned brightly, and she knew talent when she heard it. She heard it that night in Sudbury.

The moment was fraught with drama: a darkened concert hall, a very young woman with all eyes focused on her, and the perfect song for evoking heartbreak and catharsis. The classic tune, a Hank Williams gem, was "I'm So Lonesome I Could Cry." Believe it or not, the tune was not one of Hank's forty Top 40 hits. It had, however, cracked the top twenty for football quarterback Terry Bradshaw in 1976, who had turned his grid-iron fame and Southern roots into a side career in movies and music.

Shania had heard Bradshaw's version of the song on the radio, and she was also aware of Hank's version. But that night she made it her own. It was as if all the joys and hardships of her young life came pouring out of her. Mary, who stood in the wings waiting for her turn onstage, saw in Shania not only the future of country music but also her own past, a reminder of her own fading dream.

Caught in that moment, as a lightning bolt of emotion passed through Mary's heart, she quietly wiped away tears. When she spoke to Sharon about the vast potential she saw in Shania, there was no doubting her sincerity. A heart-felt bond was made that night, although it was one that would later turn bittersweet for Mary Bailey. Sharon and Mary agreed to stay in touch, with the idea that someday Mary might become Shania's manager.

In the interim Sharon continued to act as guardian of Shania's career. It was she who'd urged Shania to go onstage in the first place, and she always took an active role in what her daughter wore, sang, said, and did before an audi-ence. Shania's parents were devoted to country music, and she heard all the popular C&W artists while growing up. Tammy Wynette, George Jones, Loretta Lynn, Charley Pride, Charlie Rich, Mel Tillis, Conway Twitty, Johnny Cash, Dolly Parton, Merle Haggard, Waylon Jennings, and Buck Owens make the short list of the country giants Shania listened to when she was young, and she looks to them all as role models. "I think we got into a period where maybe people thought there were limits. But the people from that period of country music had no limitations . . . And they're as country as it gets; it doesn't get any more country than Tammy Wynette or Johnny Cash," Shania said in an interview with Gary Graff for *Country Song Roundup*.

But there was at least one element of Shania's musical growth that broke free of what her parents had in mind. The fact is, country music wasn't the only sound that came out of Shania's speakers. She was drawn to all sorts of music, including classical, so long as melody and harmony were part of the mix. Among her favorites were Stevie Wonder, Elton John, the Supremes, the Jackson 5, the Carpenters, and the Bee Gees. Shania recalls, "At 10 years old, I'd go to bed and pray, 'Please, I want Stevie Wonder to hear me sing and I want to write songs.'" She also loved the Mamas and the Papas, a passion she didn't lose as an adult. She took part in their 1998 induction into the Rock and Roll Hall of Fame.

A person who judges music by labels might scoff at these artists based on some macho prejudice against "soft pop," but when it comes to the craft of writing songs, you won't find much better this side of Hank Williams himself. "The many different styles of music I was exposed to as a child not only influenced my vocal style but, even more so, my writing style," Shania has said.

Inspired by the sweet, earthy voice of Karen Carpenter ("Her voice is just like silk, it is so gorgeous!"), the joyful yet intense rhythm of Stevie Wonder, and the melodic genius of Elton John, Shania put them into her mixed bag of influences and gave it a shake. This is a trait she shares with Dwight Yoakam—again going back to the Beatles/Buck Owens link—who has said he looks to sixties pop radio for inspiration. "When I was growing up I could hear Johnny Cash in front of Sonny & Cher," is how he put it in *Country Song Roundup*. That period of radio history played a big part in Shania's development, too, as she confirms: "We had a multiformat radio station in our hometown. I heard *everything* through radio . . ."

Shania takes an openhearted approach to music: no preset ideas about who she should be listening to or learning from, just a passion for great songwriting. Sharon and Jerry made sure Shania's musical roots were planted in country soil, but she's no hothouse flower. Her music touches all types of listeners, and she takes pride in the variety of influences that are present in her songs. "It's more across-the-board; it's not prejudiced. Hopefully, it's just entertaining," she told Brian Mansfield in a *New Country* article.

On the list of Shania's worries, the fans come right at the top, while the critics are down near the bottom. That doesn't make the buzz of their negative voices less annoying. A few writers have tried to hold up Shania's assimilation of pop music as a shortcoming on her part, as evidence that she isn't true country.

Garth Brooks delivered a great line in *Rolling Stone* when an interviewer asked if he was worried what people would think of his honoring such rock influences as Boston, Kiss, and Styx. Garth replied, "I don't think anybody's gonna come out and give me flak for that, because it would only be showing their ignorance in what is good music."

The same goes for anyone who gives Shania flak for honoring Elton John or Stevie Wonder (or Van Halen, whom Shania saw as a teenager and still mentions as the best concert experience she's had). Waylon Jennings once said, "Instruments don't make country. We're entitled to a heavy rock beat if it complements our songs." That includes a light-rock beat, or any other for that matter.

"It's amazing how we categorize things . . . Labels are necessary, but they're a necessary evil."
—SHANIA

It's too bad that so many folks assess music on the basis of labels and categories, with "pop" being used as a negative epithet. It's useful to describe music according to stylistic features, but it's stupid to use those categories to dismiss an artist's work. In an article by Joe Jackson of *The Irish Times*, Shania asserted that "fans maybe more than critics are very open-minded . . . They just tune in to the music, at whatever level, and don't care too much about labels like 'country' or 'pop.' I certainly don't."

It's perhaps a natural inclination to judge music based on categories (pop, country, punk, rap, disco, whatever), but there are more important things: for example the hook, which is like the soul, the inspiration, of the song. The difference between an artist's best and worst songs is rarely a matter of style; it's the quality of the hooks. You can insert a great hook into a song of any style and the essence will be the same.

In this area Shania's songs stack up with the best you'll ever hear. She has made the comment, "I believe you could take the music of almost anything on *Come on Over* and set it, musically, five different ways and it would still be the same song, though it may appeal to a different ear. But it will appeal to the same mind." In other words, at its root, if a listener is open-minded, Shania and Mutt's work has an appeal that goes beyond labels.

Lyrics are another big factor, although critics usually overweigh the importance of words because that's the aspect of a song that is easiest to analyze. An inspired musical hook is better felt than talked about, so the critics tend to turn most of their attention to the lyrics.

Shania's lyrics are down-to-earth and clever, based on everyday experiences that most folks can appreciate. Of course the critics don't rave about Shania's lyrics because she isn't overtly political, self-consciously artsy, or hard-bitten cool. "Worst of all, the lyrics are not only stupid clichés, they're aggressively stupid clichés," is how a *Boston Phoenix* writer described *Come on Over*.

The thing of it is, most of Shania's songs are meant to stir feelings—love, joy, comfort, pleasure . . . all those heartfelt "stupid clichés"—and it's silly to abstract the words from the music as if this were comparative literature class. The critics filter Shania's work through the distorted lens of a jaded perspective and are blind to the virtues that millions of her fans see so easily. Kix Brooks of Brooks & Dunn hit the nail on the head when he told *New Country*, "The critics get on us sometimes, but they seem to have a different agenda than the audience. A lot of times in reviews you'll see the classic line, 'but the crowd seemed to like it.' Hahaha . . . like that means nothing. Thousands of people on their feet screaming, yet the writer can't seem to understand why."

One more thing about this issue of labels and categories. The shift from Nashville being 95 percent a man's world to being more equal for women is a big reason why country music doesn't sound like it once did. The guys have years of tradition to guide (and inhibit) them, but the gals are still in the process of bustin' down walls and finding their own way. Female artists are often more creative and diverse than their male counterparts when given the chance to define their own terms. The gals are making a variety of country that's a bit unfamiliar, and not everyone has been quick to catch on.

In her teens Shania went from being just a singer to writing songs as well. "I think my delivery is more intimate, more sincere, when I'm not singing someone else's songs," she told Lucinda Chodan in a 1995 *Country* article. Shania was speaking then of the transition from her debut album to *The Woman in Me*, but the concept was no less true when she was young. In the late 1970s she was just starting to look for her own songwriting voice, her own style. It was a sign of things to come, but in the interim her career was still her mom's project as much as it was Shania's.

Sharon arranged for Shania to be on Canadian television, setting up gigs on *Opry North*, *The Mercey Brothers Show*, and *The Tommy Hunter Show*, among others. Shania recalls that Glen Campbell headlined on one of the shows she was on. He was one of the many artists of the era who fused country with pop—his 1975 hit "Rhinestone Cowboy" made it to number one on both charts. A jack-of-all-trades, Glen was a studio musician for Elvis, Frank Sinatra, and the Monkees, and he even played bass for the Beach Boys.

Another time Shania appeared on a TV show on which Ronnie Milsap was the feature guest. Born blind, he was a multi-instrument virtuoso who, from 1976 through 1987, scored twenty-nine number-one country hits, several of which crossed over to the pop charts. On one of the shows Shania recalls singing the classic "Walk on By," which had been a major crossover hit for LeRoy Van Dyke some four years before Shania was born. "Boy, would I ever like to see tapes of those shows again!" Shania told Larry Delaney in *Country Music News*.

On an episode of TNN's *Prime Time Country* after the release of her third album, Shania told a story of the time she was taking a train to Toronto for a TV appearance. At some point it dawned on her that she was riding in the wrong direction, but the conductor told her the next station was six hours away. "I said, 'You've got to stop the train right now because I'm going to be on TV,'" recalled Shania. "So they let me off in the middle of the bush with my guitar, like a little hobo." After a half hour or so she caught a train going the other way.

In the course of her early career Shania also sang in talent contests in various Ontario cities. Sharon was stung by her daughter's failure to win in a contest in her home province. "Mom was so discouraged. She couldn't understand why her little girl was never able to win a contest," Shania told Delaney. It turns out that Shania and Sharon came home happy after a long trip to British Columbia, as Shania took first place in three categories of a contest there. It is one of the major highlights of her musical résumé.

With mother and daughter both setting full sail for stardom, the job of steadying the rudder was left to dad. Jerry was a pragmatic man, and they trusted him to keep the pursuit of dreams from capsizing the entire family. Shania expressed it to Barbara Hager like this: "He made decisions about whether it made sense to drive somewhere to perform for free or pay the heating bill that week."

By the time Shania was in her late teens, the family finances were improving. Jerry was able to

salt away the money it took to start his own reforestation business. Jerry and his crew were
hired to plant seeds and saplings in parts of the
bush where loggers had cut down trees. Shania
could often be found helping with the business,
and soon she was leading a crew of workers. An
excerpt from her bio in the *Country Music Encyclopedia* reveals that what she was doing was no mere
nature walk:

> I was foreman with a 13-man crew, many of
> whom were Indians. I'd run the crew and
> we'd plant trees through the summer. We'd
> get up between 4 and 6 in the morning, live
> on beans, bread and tea, walk [for] up to an
> hour to the site and work there all day with
> no shelter in rain, snow or sunshine, in the
> middle of the bush, hours from civilization. I
> did that for five years. It was very hard work,
> but I loved it.

It's easy to see that taking on such a respon-
sibility would give a young woman great confidence. Shania was getting a real-world education
about taking care of business and working with
people—not to mention learning how to handle
a chain saw! Her vocal talents came in handy,
too: she remembers singing out loud as a way
to ward off curious bears who might wander
into camp.

Shania was in the woods for weeks at a time, and being removed from the distractions of the modern world gave her the chance to write songs when she wasn't working. "It was so secluded that you would not dare to put any fragrance on you. This meant no soap and definitely no perfume, otherwise the mosquitoes would eat you alive," she recalls. "I would sit alone in the forest with my dog and a guitar and just write songs."

When she wasn't onstage or working, Shania attended Timmins High and Vocational School. She had a reputation for being a nice but serious person; a teenager like most others but with a deeper sense of what she wanted for her life in the long run. Her free time was spent singing, doing chores at home, and trying to earn extra money. She even worked for a while at the local McDonald's. With all that on her plate, Shania made time for her homework and some in-school socializing, but that was about it. She wasn't out trying to scam beer on the weekends or cutting class on sunny days. Her sights were set on the future.

Shania was something of a tomboy as a youngster. When her body started to fill out she became very self-conscious. "I saw at school that if you had breasts and you bounced and you were feminine, that everyone paid attention only to that. I *hated* that," Shania explained in *Country Weekly*.

Later she came to realize that she shouldn't have to hide behind layers of loose clothing just to insulate herself from other people's hang-ups. "I realize now that I should have been proud of the fact that I was female, and tried to change their perceptions instead of changing myself."

As much of a focal point as singing was for her, it's interesting that Shania's classmates weren't generally aware of her aspirations. She recalls, "A friend of mine in high school asked me once, 'Is it true that you play in a band at night and that you went to do *The Tommy Hunter Show?*' It was like I had to make this confession. I said, 'I've got to tell you, I'm a singer,' and she said, 'Well, I just don't believe you. I've known you all this time, and I don't believe you're a singer.'" By the time she graduated, her friends did know about her aspirations; in fact there is a grainy black-and-white photo in the school's 1982–83 yearbook of her singing. As for her graduation ceremony, Shania wasn't able to attend.

Instead she was on the road with her band, the Longshot. She had joined the group after they saw her singing on a local telethon. The band had been so impressed by Shania's voice that they sought her out and asked her to join, and over time she grew to be an essential part of the act. To this day she still has a black ledger that the drummer gave her. He suggested she stop keeping her songs on loose pieces of paper, so she rewrote all her work into the ledger and kept it with her. "I look back at that book and I look at all the different handwriting I've had over the years," she told Wray Ellis of *Country Wave.* "It went from being really neat to really messy."

The Longshot was primarily a rock and roll cover band; they worked the current radio hits and a few classics. They played tunes by Foreigner, Crosby, Stills, Nash and Young, and A Flock of Seagulls. If it was a hit, they would play it, but country music wasn't part of the program. With hard work and time the Longshot grew into a tight little band, and they enjoyed a measure of success within the confines of Timmins. "We were pretty good actually," Shania recalled in *FHM* magazine, "pretty dangerous for my hometown . . ." The venues where they played were usually packed to capacity when the Longshot hit the stage.

Shania was a compelling front person, the sixteen-year-old female lead singer in a hot local rock band. It was an exciting time for her, performing in bars she wasn't legally allowed to frequent. Alcohol wasn't a temptation for Shania, due in part to the fact that, when she was thirteen, her parents taught her a valuable lesson. Jerry and Sharon weren't heavy drinkers but on a holiday they were tipping back a few. The curious Shania wanted a taste, so her dad let her have a sip. She told him she liked it, so he let her drink enough that she got sick and was hungover the next morning. The family gave her comfort until she felt better, then "made great fun" of her in the weeks that followed. Getting drunk held little romantic appeal for Shania after that. She never drank—she was too intent on her singing—but she did cut loose and get the crowds rockin' with her stage presence. If things got too rowdy in front of the stage, she didn't hesitate to jump in and break up fights. "I'm surprised I didn't get myself killed," she marvels. Shania's fashion sense was purely of the period: tons of black eyeliner, big frizzy hair, and black satin jackets with embroidery.

Being in a band is like being married. The hours spent practicing and planning and performing demand a big investment of time, and the emotional involvement of creative collaboration is intense. The expectations and egos can make for a mix that explodes rather than percolates. The Longshot built up a decent local following—there are still some people in Timmins who remember the band—and they also did some regional touring. But in the end they split up, in part over artistic differences and in part because of a sneaking suspicion that they'd reached their peak. In a *Maclean's* article by Brian D. Johnson, Shania came out with one of the all-time great quotes about the feeling of postgig letdown, saying she always wound up walking back home "alone at 3 A.M. with a rock in my pocket."

Not long after Shania had completed her studies, Sharon phoned Mary Bailey and asked her to take over as her daughter's manager. The timing was right for Mary, who wanted to stay plugged into the country music business even though she was no longer singing. Sharon trusted Mary and felt that Shania would benefit from her contacts and experience. Mary was seen as a trusted adviser and friend. She knew the obstacles that a young singer encounters, and she was happy to help Shania in every way possible. Mary felt a genuine affection for the spirited young Shania, and she found much to admire in Sharon.

Mary and Sharon believed that Shania needed a full-time manager who not only knew the ropes of the business but who also had Shania's best interests at heart. Shania had already been contacted by people who were eager to manage her. She'd even signed a contract and taken a trip to Nashville in an effort to attract a recording label, but not much had come of it. After agreeing to take the reins, Mary bought out the other person's contract and began pouring her energy into the talented teenager's career.

The more Mary worked with Shania, the more she came to believe that her client had enormous talent. "She had the voice of a young Tanya Tucker. She was a great artist, even at that age,"

Mary remembers. She also saw a special quality about Shania that went beyond a strong voice and youthful beauty: it was a certain look in the eyes, a spark that made her want to be the very best that she could be. If that passion could be ignited, great things were bound to happen—Mary was sure of it.

But, as fate would have it, the timing was not quite perfect for Shania. At eighteen years of age, she wasn't ready to go full tilt into the life of an aspiring country music star. Mary and Shania did take one trip to Nashville together in the hope of getting a contract, but it was again to no avail. Shortly thereafter the deal between Mary and Shania simply fizzled out. Their parting was on good terms, and they left open the option of re-uniting in the future.

❊ 5 ❊

God Bless the Children

> "I guess the thing to remember is that no matter how tough things get in your life, you still have the power to make a choice. You can fade away or you can strive to survive. I went for the striving road."
>
> —SHANIA

Barely out of high school, Shania had already amassed the know-how of a veteran performer. Clearly she was no longer the shy little girl who sang on top of lunch counters, in front of first-graders at show-and-tell, or for the after-hours patrons at the Mattagami Hotel. The years of singing at every carnival and fair, family get-together, and senior-citizen center, appearing on TV variety shows, warming up for older artists, competing in talent shows across the province, fronting her own rock-and-roll cover band—it all combined to give Shania the savvy and poise of a seasoned pro.

Of course she was also still a kid, itching to escape the small town where she'd grown up, yet not wanting to leave the safety of her family. She had made it through her high-school years without succumbing to any overly serious affairs of the heart, so a relationship wouldn't be a factor in what she decided to do or where she chose to go. In theory she was free to fly. On the other hand, Shania just wasn't ready to give up the comfort of seeing her mom, dad, brothers, and sisters every day. College wasn't in the cards, so she decided to stay in Timmins for a while longer.

Jerry's reforestation venture was going well, and Shania was a big part of the business. What's more, her presence at home kept things running smoothly when Sharon and Jerry were stretched too thin. The entire family knew the day was fast approaching when Shania would spread her wings and fly, but they also knew she'd never stray too far or be absent in times of need. Shania later proved, unfortunately in the most tragic conditions, that their faith was justified.

What her mom had set in motion, Shania took forward on her own. She kept adding to her repertoire, splitting time between rock and country, and she cemented the resolve to make a name for herself as a singer. By the time she was nineteen Shania's hard work and desire had begun to pay small but solid dividends.

In the winter of 1984 her name was mentioned

in a *Country Music News* article. The story focused on Toronto-based producer Stan Campbell's projects for the year ahead. He raved about her potential, saying, "Eileen [as Shania was known] possesses a powerful voice with an impressive range," and "she has the necessary drive, ambition, and positive attitude to achieve her goals." There was even a photograph of Shania to go along with the article. It was the first notch in her belt in terms of media attention, and Shania was thrilled.

What came next was even more of a boost for the still-teenage singer. One of the projects Campbell had put together involved a little-known Canadian singer named Tim Denis, who was cutting tracks for his debut album. Campbell took Shania into the studio and put her to work singing backup on a song titled "Heavy on the Sunshine." It wasn't a ticket to the high life for Shania, but it was nevertheless a watershed moment in her career.

It also set the scene for her next foray into the studio, roughly a year later, in January of 1985. A producer named Tony Migliore was working on an album for Canadian artist Kelita Haverland at Chelsea Studios in Nashville. It so happened that Shania was in Music City taping demos at that time. One thing led to another—her strong voice and previous brush with studio backup singing were key—and she ended up doing backup vocals for Kelita. When the record was released by RCA, it scored a minor hit with the title track, "Too Hot to Handle."

You've probably heard the old saw about how the further along you get, the more you see how far you've got to go. That's sure true of the music business, where each small success shows you just how distant fame and fortune really are. Shania was about to learn this firsthand. For all the work she'd done, for all the progress she was making, she was still quite a distance away from getting her own record deal.

In the years since high school Shania had done some touring, some recording, and a lot of dreaming about the future. Yet deep down she knew something was holding her back: the small-town girl inside her, the one who flinched at the idea of moving out of Timmins and away from her family. The time had come to break free from childhood, from security, from the life she'd always known. The place where she needed to be was obvious, the only option possible when you got down to brass tacks: Toronto.

The capital city of Ontario is also show-business central in Canada. With its Broadway shows and world-class symphony and jumpin' nightspots, Toronto truly comes alive after dark. Country music has a big fan base in Canada, and the brain trust resides in Toronto. It's where the cash and the contacts come together to make or break aspiring Canadian country music stars.

Shania got right to work building her new life in the big city. Her day job consisted of secretarial duty at a computer school, but in the evenings and on weekends she poured all her energies into music. She rehearsed and performed in a variety of situations, with bands of varying styles and talent. She sometimes was able to showcase her own writing but was best known for her versatility and skill at interpreting other people's songs. Perhaps the peak moment of Shania's tenure in Toronto came when she was picked to open for musical-theater legend Bernadette Peters, who was doing a show with the Toronto Symphony Orchestra.

Again, the small tastes of sweet success were both a sign that she was on the right track and a milepost telling her that the ultimate goal was still out of view. Shania loved living in the city most of the time. She made contacts with people from all walks of life and all parts of the country, got dressed to the nines for many of her shows, and savored her independence. But she also missed her family and frequently had to fend off feelings of frustration and isolation. Letters and phone calls helped fill the gap, but it wasn't the same as having a shoulder to cry on.

Shania was actually happy to get back up to Timmins during the spring and summer to resume her spot on Jerry's crew. She put in her usual sweat and blood in the bush and then, as she explains it, "after a summer of northern exposure, from the treacherous June blackflies to an August hailstorm, I'd go back to Toronto and slip into my sequined gown again."

Back in the big city for the fall of 1987, the twenty-two-year-old chanteuse got back to work on her career. She had no way to know that everything she'd built up to that point was about to be ripped out from under her by cruel fate, no way to foresee how her entire life was about to change in an instant.

November 1, 1987, a winter Sunday that seemed like any other. The telephone rang, Shania picked up. At the other end was her older sister, Jill, speaking in a clipped tone. Clearly this was to be no casual call, and Shania felt a wave of sick fear as she hoped the worst wasn't true. But it was, the very worst was true: Jerry and Sharon Twain were dead.

Shania's parents had been driving back from one of the reforestation sites, on what was planned to be one of their last such trips of the year, when the Chevy Suburban they were driving crashed head-on with a logging truck. The end was instantaneous. As Shania later explained it in *Maclean's*, "All they heard was a horn." Youngest brother Mark was in the truck when the wreck occurred, and the experience was understandably traumatic for him. In a 1996 interview with Robert K. Oermann, Shania said, "He's been in and out of school a lot since my parents died. He is still searching."

How can anyone understand how these children felt? Shania's heart was cast adrift, cut loose from its moorings and alone at sea. What words could possibly describe the sense of loss? And as if the tragedy needed compounding, there was irony involved. The logging truck, a symbol of the muscle and soul the family had put into their business, wouldn't have been on the road if not for a recent change in the law that had restricted Sunday trucking on Ontario highways. Shania told Larry Delaney in *Country Music News*, "It shouldn't have happened."

It shouldn't have, but it had. In that one terrible flash two cherished people were gone forever and a gaping hole was torn in the lives of Shania and her siblings. Is there a sadder word in the English language than "orphan"? It was impossible to imagine a world where Jerry and Sharon were no longer available to give advice and comfort, but such a world was now a stark reality.

Shania sensed that the plans she'd put into motion were screeching to a stop, and she saw her life taking a very different path than she would have ever pictured it taking. Shock and grief quickly mingled with worry. Neighbors, friends, and extended family offered what they could in the way of help, but after the funeral services had come and gone and the rest of the world steamed ahead, what would become of Carrie-Ann, Mark, and Darryl, all of whom still lived at home?

Jill had long since gotten married and moved away, and she had kids of her own to look after. None of the extended family was in a position to take in three new members. The entire weight was bearing down on Shania like a freight train comin' 'round the bend, and she could feel the tracks shaking as it rumbled toward her. Her first impulse, born of anguish and panic, was to bolt: "I wanted to escape it all and go off to Africa," she confided to Barbara Hager.

The impulse to escape, to flee from what was coming, hit fast and hard but didn't stick. Shania just isn't the type to run, never has been. She let go of the life she'd started in Toronto and moved back home. She learned what she had to about death taxes. She had some idea of what her dad's equipment was worth, and she sold it off to pay the mortgage and the bills. It was up to Shania to keep the family together, and that's exactly what she did.

With oldest sister Jill on her own, and youngest sister Carrie-Ann eighteen and able to look after herself for the most part (Shania still took on the dad's role of screening boyfriends), the bulk of the task would lie in raising two young brothers who had lost their parents. Mark and Darryl were only fourteen and thirteen, respectively—tough ages in the best of times, and these were not those. Both boys would be dealing with grief and upset on top of the usual adolescent growing pains, and their sister Shania was to be their surrogate parent, their new figure of authority. "She was really strict with us," Mark later recalled. "She was scared."

With no advance warning, Shania had lost her beloved parents and was raising two teenage boys. "It was like being thrown into the deep end of a pool and just having to swim," she explained in *People.* She remembers that there were times when money was in such short supply that they wound up washing their clothes in a stream, rather than spend quarters at the local Laundromat. Kneeling in that cold brook as she scrubbed shirts and jeans by hand is a memory Shania isn't trying to forget. "That's a part of me I want to try and keep," she told Johanna Schneller in *Maclean's.* "I think it keeps things in perspective."

That is an overriding theme in Shania's life: keeping things in perspective. She loves to "get totally crazy" and "have a little fun," as one of her songs suggests, but she is also very down-to-earth. She takes after Jerry in that respect. Shania learned to accept change at an early age, and at this point there isn't anything she can't handle. "I think that if you are ever in a desperate situation and you can get through it, you have a confidence in life that you would otherwise not have," she once told *The Toronto Sun*'s Jane Stevenson. "I realize that no matter what I ever lose, I'll be able to manage."

Pluck and grit notwithstanding, it's tough to manage without help, and Shania was in dire need. She was facing what she later called "the hardest time of my life," and she didn't want to give up all her dreams of a career in music. But what could she do? With two teenage boys under her wings it was practically impossible to take flight as an artist. "I had responsibilities, so I couldn't just go around getting gigs here or there, or writing only when I felt like it," she later recounted. It looked like her career might be over before it started.

In search of a beacon to guide her through the darkness, Shania called on her friend and former manager Mary Bailey. It was the wisest move she could have made—Mary still believed in Shania's abilities and was very much prepared to offer an encouraging word. "You have great talent," Mary assured Shania. Mary vividly recalled the way Shania had brought her to tears that night long ago with a stirring version of "I'm So Lonesome I Could Cry." Although she'd never have wished it to be under such sad circumstances, in some ways it felt like destiny that Shania was back in Mary's life.

Mary had a solution that would help get Shania's career back on track and provide a way for her to support the family. Located in the town of Huntsville, some two and a half hours from Toronto by car, was a century-old resort called Deerhurst. Mary set up an audition for Shania with the producers of a Las Vegas–style revue there. Even though they weren't actively looking for a lead singer, they were so impressed by Shania's demo tape and audition that they ended up making a special place for her. "She was *that* good," explained producer Lynn Foster in *Country Weekly*.

Shania didn't hesitate when the people at Deerhurst offered her a spot in their *Viva Vegas* show. She sold the house in Timmins, packed up her siblings and trucked them to Huntsville, rented a little house just outside of town, and settled in. After a while the family got back into some semblance of a normal routine, but it could never be the same without Jerry and Sharon. "At the time you couldn't help but feel sorry for her," recalls Lynn Foster.

It was all that Shania could do to take care of Mark and Darryl's daily needs and still keep her act sharp at Deerhurst. She divvied up the household chores and tried to make sure that Mark and Darryl stayed out of trouble. She drove them to ball games and school dances, made sure they were healthy and well fed—in short she took on all the tasks of a single parent, which included bringing home the bacon from Deerhurst.

Shania saw the resort as more than just a source of income: it was a training ground, a musical university where she could work with producers and other performers and be put to the test by a different audience every night. She learned choreographic routines and other elements of stage work. "I always had a dream of going to performing arts school . . . that's what Deerhurst gave me," she told Barbara Hager. What's more, the music became an escape from the lingering sadness over Jerry and Sharon's passing and from the burden of raising her two brothers.

The shows at Deerhurst were a hodgepodge of styles. On any given evening Shania might do a medley of Motown classics, a disco pick such as the Village People's "YMCA," a bit of George Gershwin's old-time pop standards and Andrew Lloyd Webber's show tunes, Latin numbers, plus a selection of Top 40 hits. One of the highlights came when she belted out "Somewhere Over the Rainbow," clad in a stunning green gown. "That was a knockout number," Lynn Foster recalls. Shania did some of her songs as a solo act and others as one part of an over-the-top group extravaganza.

She could tackle any song in the book and deliver it with verve. It made no difference whether the audience was a busload of French tourists, a convention of Windsor auto-industry execs, or a garden-club get-together; she never failed to entertain. The crowds at Deerhurst were generally attentive, but Shania took them that extra step from mere politeness to captivation. She was *that* good, and it was no secret that her talent was bigger than the venue. "She had aspirations and she knew she was going somewhere with her career," Lynn Foster remarked in a *Country Weekly* article written by Wendy Newcomer.

At home the going was a lot tougher and a lot less glitzy. It was during this time that the water well ran dry at the house where they were living. "We went down to the river with five-gallon jugs," she told John Keyes. "That's how we'd flush the toilets." But the Twain kids did their best to keep each other strong, and most of the time Shania and her brothers were happy and content. "They were going through so much," Shania has said of Mark and Darryl. "I was just concerned about them." The sibling bonds that already existed between them grew even more unbreakable during the three years in Huntsville.

By the summer of 1991, when Shania turned twenty-six, Mark and Darryl were all but set to leave the nest. Years later, in a press release put out by Mercury-Nashville, Shania expressed just how liberated she'd felt when the time finally arrived: "I felt like a 45-year-old woman whose kids had gone away to college. I was like '*Wow!*' I have my whole life to live now. I said 'now what am I gonna do with my life?' I decided I wanted to go for it!"

Once again she turned to her old friend Mary Bailey. It was clear to Mary that the spark she'd seen in Shania as a teen now burned as a full-on flame. While she was convinced that Shania was hungry to go as far as talent and hard work could take her, Mary needed to be assured that Shania was devoted to country music.

As a performer, Mary knew all about pushing country to its limits, but she had always stayed true to the genre. She wanted to know that it was Shania's intention to follow that path, too. In her heart she already knew the answer. "She was raised on it . . . she's very 'rootsy,'" is how Mary once assessed Shania's connection to country. With that settled, Mary got down to the task of helping Shania push her career to a higher level.

One of the first moves was a name change. Not that there was anything wrong with "Eileen," but it lacked juice. "When I first got started," Shania later recalled, "they were calling me 'Arleen,' 'Irene,' 'Elaine,' everything but Eileen." The question of what should replace the name she'd gone by her entire life was not an easy one. As it happens, the answer came right out of the dressing room at Deerhurst. A wardrobe assistant at the resort had a beautiful Ojibwa name that also had a special meaning: "I'm on my way." Shania has said that at first she didn't know about the name's translation; someone else told her what it meant in English. "I thought that it was such a beautiful name and I could really relate to it," she has said. With her new freedom and new name, Eileen was reborn as Shania. It was perfect. After all, this time she truly was on her way.

She gave notice at Deerhurst and began putting her things in order for a move back to Timmins. Shania intended to immerse herself in country music and prepare for the big push into Nashville. She looked forward to going home and felt anxious to begin the new chapter in her life. But before she said so long to Huntsville, she was to experience one very important evening at Deerhurst.

Shania had recorded a new demo tape, which Mary then sent out to her contacts on Music Row in Nashville. While she wasn't what you'd call a music-industry heavyweight—a power broker who could make things happen with a snap of her fingers—Mary Bailey did have a little pull. She had worked the country music life for quite a while as a singer, and she'd charmed most of the people who met her along the way. Folks who knew Mary knew that she could be trusted.

One of the friends Mary contacted on Shania's behalf was a Nashville lawyer named Richard Frank. A founding member of the Country Music Association, his opinion carried plenty of weight in Music City. When she spoke to him on the phone, Mary enthused about how her protégée was ripe for a move to the big time. "Just listen to the tape," she urged him.

Frank did listen to Shania's demo, and what he heard was enough to convince him that a trip north of the border was in order. He and his wife came to see Shania give one of her last performances at Deerhurst, and they were simply blown away. Frank promised Mary that as soon as he got back to Nashville, he would put out the word on the street about Shania Twain. It was the catalyst for a chain reaction, the first domino to fall.

Shania went back to Timmins and took a job behind the complaints desk at Sears as a way to pay the bills and put food on the table. She was involved in a serious romance with a man named Paul Bolduc. Sadly, the relationship wasn't destined to go the distance, but Paul is credited as Shania's "saving grace" in the liner notes to her debut album. Paul's mom, Hélène Bolduc, was a cofounder of Shania's fan club in Canada; in fact, the club headquarters were once located in the basement of their house in Timmins.

In the meantime Dick Frank was being true to his promise. He touted Shania's virtues to a respected independent producer named Norro Wilson, one of Nashville's major players, a man who was well established in the music business as a singer, songwriter, and producer.

In the early 1970s Norro scored three Top 40 hits on the country charts as a singer. He also penned hits for artists such as Tammy Wynette and Charlie Rich. Norro's production credits included working with the legendary Ray Price on *Sometimes a Rose* (arguably the best of Ray's 1990s efforts). He helped restart Charley Pride's career in 1982 with his work on *Charley Sings Everybody's Choice*. In short this was the person who could jump-start Shania's career. (He later did the same thing for Mindy McCready.)

Norro's interest in the fledgling Canadian was high. He agreed to produce a three-song demo to showcase Shania for the reps at major labels. The job at Sears didn't pay enough to cover the expense of a stay in Nashville, not to mention the cost of Norro Wilson's time and expertise. Once again Mary Bailey came to the rescue, footing the bill to enable Shania to follow her dream. "My dad was making his money and my mom was spending it on this dream," Mary's son Robert Kasner was quoted in *Three Chords and the Truth*.

It was all clicking into place at a rapid pace for Shania. Norro Wilson brought the demo to the attention of various A&R execs. Among them was Buddy Cannon of Mercury-Nashville, who passed the tape along to Mercury senior vice-president Harold Shedd, who then sent it to Luke Lewis, the president of Mercury-Nashville. "That was it!" as

Shania later put it. She signed a contract and began preparing to cut her first album.

The first step was to relocate, this time to Music City, U.S.A. It was just too stressful for Shania to be hauling herself from Timmins to Nashville all the time, and the label was urging her to be available on short notice. Heaven knew there was plenty for her to do: recording, promotions, photo shoots, etc. The good folks at Sears would just have to find someone new to stand behind their complaints desk.

Slated to coproduce Shania's debut CD were Norro Wilson and Harold Shedd. An artist couldn't hope for a more impressive twosome as far as Nashville credentials go. Back in 1980 Shedd produced the first number-one single for Alabama, the most famous country band in the world. Wilson and Shedd had amassed several decades of studio time between them, and they brought all that combined experience to *Shania Twain*, the album. The team seemed geared for sure-fire chart success, but the album's sales ended up sputtering because Wilson and Shedd also brought old-school preconceptions about how to make a country recording. And, at least in Shania's situation, the formula didn't fly.

One of Nashville's hallowed traditions is the division of labor between the songwriters, the instrumentalists, and the singers. "Let the pros do what they do best" is the attitude that prevails, and it frequently works to perfection. In the case of *Shania Twain*, it didn't. Only one of the ten compositions is a Shania original, the feisty "God Ain't Gonna Getcha for That" (a reference to the 1975 George Jones and Tammy Wynette hit "God's Gonna Get'cha"). Cowritten with Kent Robbins, Shania's song is by far the album's best. The other nine tunes are all competent but unremarkable Nashville fare. Words such as "tepid" and "pedestrian" have been used to describe *Shania Twain*. Thom Owens, in the *All Music Guide to Country*, summed up most people's thoughts on the effort:

> Shania Twain's eponymous debut album was a bland set of contemporary country that demonstrated her considerable vocal abilities but none of the spark that informed her breakthrough, *The Woman in Me*. Part of the problem is that none of the songs is well constructed, and each leans toward soft-rock instead of country or country-rock. By and large, the songs lack strong melodies, so they have to rely on Twain's vocal skills; she is too showy to make any of these mediocre songs stick. It's a promising debut, largely because it showcases her fine vocal skills, but it isn't engaging enough to be truly interesting outside of a historical context.

That "too showy" comment—somewhat ironic in light of Shania's childhood fear of being called a show-off—isn't entirely off base. But again, the problem is those "mediocre songs," which are too plain and pat to offer a suitable showcase for Shania's charisma and sense of drama. It's like seeing a runway model at the local hardware store—she ends up coming across as "too showy," when the real problem is simply the drabness of the surroundings. Shania is careful not to denigrate her first album, but she doesn't consider it her best work either: "I don't hate the album, but I'm better singing songs I write."

It goes without saying that everyone involved in the project had great expectations for *Shania Twain*. And it isn't as if the album was a total flop; it has since been certified gold in the U.S., with over 500,000 copies sold. But those numbers were given a huge boost by the later success of *The Woman in Me*. At the time of its release *Shania Twain* didn't make a big splash, selling in the neighborhood of 100,000 copies.

It wasn't from lack of effort. Mercury put a lot of care and brainpower into the marketing strategy for Shania's first album. Still flush from a Billy Ray Cyrus/"Achy, Breaky Heart" grand slam the year before, Mercury was itching to duplicate its success. Harold Shedd had signed Billy Ray in the summer of 1990, although his debut record, *Some Gave All*, didn't reach the streets until mid-1992. When it hit, it hit like a tsunami.

Months before its release, *Some Gave All* was primed for the big time by a ton of advance press and a video for "Achy, Breaky Heart" that featured hunky Billy Ray wiggling to one of the most infectious musical hooks ever conceived, doing a dance step that caught on as the line-dance sensation of the year. The album debuted at number one on the pop charts, the first country record ever to do so.

Mercury head Luke Lewis and company saw Shania's visual-promo potential—actually, it was hard to miss—and they set out to make the most of it. The idea was to get Shania's name on the Nashville grapevine ahead of the release date for *Shania Twain* so that the press would spread the word to country music fans that a new star was on the horizon.

The album's first single, an upbeat little piece of candy called "What Made You Say That," was accompanied by a playful and sexy video shot on a Miami beach. The basic theme: Shania frolics on the seashore with a tanned and shirtless hunk. The song failed to make waves on the country charts, but the video later turned out to be a watermark in Shania's life and career for reasons she never anticipated.

Mercury didn't put all their eggs in the video basket. The label assembled a trio of its newest artists—John Brannen, Toby Keith, and Shania—and put together a promotion dubbed the Triple Play. It included a CD sampler and a video sampler of the three artists, plus a special concert tour of sixteen cities. It was all moving so fast—Mary and Shania were scrambling to keep pace.

Mary fielded hundreds of phone calls from reporters, promoters, and assorted folks in the business. Shania was tickled pink by the attention, but she also found that being caught in the starmaker machine had a downside. She couldn't help missing the bush and the freedom and peace of mind it offered her. It was in her blood to "jump in my truck and get lost in the woods," as she explained to Larry Delaney. A person can plan and dream for something all her life, but it never comes out exactly the way she imagines.

It probably isn't exaggerating by much to say that there are singers who would give their right arm for the opportunity Shania had been given. She was well aware of this, saying at the time, "I guess I'd better not complain about being lonely." And of course she never dreamed of turning back. But the longing she felt did confirm that someday she was bound to exit the bright lights of Nashville and head back to the forest, where she felt most at home.

That lonely feeling was fueled in part by the mixed results that the Triple Play tour yielded, with Shania coming out neither on the wrong nor the right end of the measuring stick. Toby Keith's album produced a number-one hit with "Should've Been a Cowboy," plus a couple of other top-five hits. John Brannen's album failed to make much impact at all. *Shania Twain* fell somewhere in the middle, which unfortunately doesn't really "pay the fiddler" in the dog-eat-dog world of modern country music.

It was the atmosphere of compete-or-go-home that made the Triple Play seem to be an error in judgment in retrospect. Picture the nightmare logistics and the bruised egos you'd create by putting three new artists—each trying to make a name for him- or herself—in a battle for the same audience, the same space, and the same label resources. Label mates or not, Toby Keith, John Brannen, and Shania were fighting for their careers, and each sensed that at least one would likely fall by the wayside. A few years after both Shania and Toby hit the big time, Toby told *The Calgary Sun*, "I thought she was very talented and she's great on stage. But what surprised me later was that she was such a good writer."

In the effort to separate *Shania Twain* from the pack, Mary, Shania, and the reps at Mercury came up with an intriguing idea for the album's cover art, which was shot in a northern Ontario location that Shania scouted in her grandpa's snowshoes. It features a trained wolf named Cane, who was transported from Vancouver for the photo session. The pictures show Shania, bundled in buckskin and denim, standing with Cane by a blue-and-gold fire in the foreground of frozen tundra. The icy expanse is like an alien landscape, made all the more stark by the presence of a bright-eyed young woman and an equally bright-eyed wolf. The exotic locale certainly conveys the idea that Shania isn't just another act from Nashville.

In addition to the recording and promo work for her album, Shania found time to make a contribution on Sammy Kershaw's *Haunted Heart*. She is one of four people credited with doing background vocals on the album, and she can be heard singing harmonies on "Still Lovin' You" and "What Might Have Been." She also sings backup on Jeff Chance's 1992 album, *Walk Softly on the Bridges*.

In April of 1993 Shania's self-titled first album became available in stores. That in itself is noteworthy when you think about how far she traveled in such a short span of time. In one year she went from doing a variety act in Ontario to having her own Nashville-produced album in retail stores across the U.S. and Canada, and even in Europe. Whatever might occur in the future, she had already come further than most ever do.

Shania is aware that there are worthy singers who struggle for years and never get such an opportunity. In a sense she had worked all her life for the moment, and when she knocked on the door to Nashville, it simply opened wide and welcomed her inside. "There must have just been a space for me," she once said in *Interview* magazine.

Trouble was, for all the energy and hope that the company poured into *Shania Twain*, for all the talk of a Billy Ray Cyrus–type breakthrough, the album just didn't make it with the folks who buy country music. See, the market is driven by hit singles. Nine times out of ten an album that consists of all B-grade songs will be outsold by one that contains mostly C's mixed with one or two A's.

It's those A-grade songs—the ones that make it onto radio playlists and then get stuck in people's heads—that push album sales. The first single from *Shania Twain* topped out at number fifty-five on *Billboard*'s country chart; not bad, but far from earthshaking. The advance press, the promo tours, the sexy video—none of it matters if the song doesn't come to life in the ears and hearts of the listeners. A few U.S. markets—Salt Lake City and Denver were two of the standouts—did respond as hoped, but overall sales of the album were sluggish. It was crucial that the second single, "Dance with the One That Brought You," make a bigger impact on the charts than "What Made You Say That" had.

Such was the state of affairs when Mary Bailey got an unexpected phone call from none other than L.A.–based actor/writer/director Sean Penn. He had seen Shania's first video and wondered if she might be interested in having him direct her second. Shania was, in her own words, "jumping up and down" with excitement when she heard the news. Mary and Shania were optimistic that this would be the ticket to getting *Shania Twain* on course. Hollywood and Nashville don't hook up every day, but when they do it can be beneficial for both.

It took a little time for Sean to find a free space on his calendar, but in May of '93 filming got under way on the "Dance with the One That Brought You" video. A midtempo number with a laid-back swing feel, the song features nice pedal steel and piano work. The lyrics tell about a gal whose boyfriend likes to cut loose when he goes out; deep down she knows their love is true. Veteran character actor Charles Durning took the role of "Good Time Charlie." Shania did such a great job with her part that Sean suggested she try her hand at film acting someday.

The video shoot with Sean Penn was certainly fun and interesting—a great learning experience for Shania—but the ultimate goal was to help make "Dance" into a hit, and when push came to shove that didn't happen. The single stalled outside of the Top 40, and *Shania Twain* sales slowed to a trickle. When their third swing at a hit single— the sentimental ballad "You Lay a Whole Lot of

Love on Me" (with a video that shows Shania with big hair)—suffered a similarly lackluster fate, Mary and Shania were becoming flat worried.

And for good reason. The country music business is ruthless by nature, and patience is often in short supply. An artist may get only one chance to spend the label's cash. The record companies can pick and choose from a supply of hungry young hopefuls who are waiting to move up if someone ahead of them stumbles.

Shania wasn't necessarily stumbling; then again, her footing wasn't exactly secure.

✳ 6 ✳

Two Hearts, One Beat

> "He sees the big picture of everything, life, the whole deal ... And he respects everybody and everything about the business."
> —BRYAN WHITE

> "Mutt's a huge country music fan. I may be the princess in his life, but Tammy Wynette is the queen."
> —SHANIA

Who can pinpoint the exact formula for fulfillment—the correlation of luck, timing, hard work, vision, talent, and faith that propels us to our ultimate goals? What happened next for Shania—the event that took her off the slow train and put her on the fast track to success—was the coalescing of a lifetime's worth of luck, timing, hard work, vision, talent, and faith. It began with

95

the ring of a phone and climaxed with a ring on Shania's finger.

It seems that Mary had taken a call from a stranger who identified himself as "Mutt." He claimed to have been directed to her by Mercury-Nashville, and he was interested in talking with Shania. Having never heard of him, Mary decided this fellow with the foreign accent (he was born in South Africa and lived in England) and the unusual nickname (it was given to him in childhood) was a resourceful fan trying to sneak his way through the back door into Shania's life. Mary sent this Mr. Lange an autographed photo and assumed it would be the last contact she'd have with him.

As it turns out, the unknown caller was Robert John "Mutt" Lange, one of the world's most successful music producers and a superb songwriter to boot. This is the man who was to become the Prince Charming of Shania's life, not to mention the white knight who rescued her career. It's no wonder that Mary Bailey had never heard of Mutt Lange, since most of his work had been with rock and soul acts.

Mutt's career as a producer traces back to the late 1970s, when he worked in England with a San Francisco group known as Clover. The band's harmonica player was Huey Lewis, who later formed Huey Lewis and the News, one of the biggest rock and roll bands of the eighties. It was Mutt who wrote Huey's huge hit "Do You Believe in Love?"—a song that critic Stephen Thomas Erlewine called "a stunner, a tight set of polished, anthemic hooks that is one of the best mainstream pop singles of the early '80s." Substitute "country albums of the mid-nineties" for the last six words in the preceding sentence, and you get a near-perfect description of *The Woman in Me.*

Mutt's production work on AC/DC's 1980 rock classic *Back in Black* is legendary: pure and multifaceted and hard as a diamond. That album sold over ten million copies in the U.S., a feat that Mutt has duplicated several times since. He turned the trick twice for Def Leppard, in 1983 with *Pyromania* and four years later with *Hysteria.* Mutt has also produced hit records for Graham Parker, Foreigner, the Backstreet Boys, XTC, Michael Bolton, Billy Ocean, the Cars, and Bryan Adams.

A wizard of production, Mutt is also a master songwriter with a sharp ear for inspired hooks. "Let's be honest . . . Mutt could work with my mum and have a hit record," Bryan Adams once asserted. Mutt has won awards from the National Academy of Recording Arts and Sciences (a Grammy Award for Producer of the Year) and the American Society of Composers, Authors and Publishers (ASCAP).

His writing credits include some of the biggest hits in music history, songs such as "Please

Forgive Me" and "(Everything I Do) I Do It for You" for Bryan Adams, and "Photograph" and "Pour Some Sugar on Me" for Def Leppard. That last one has a funny story behind it that illustrates the way Mutt takes whatever comes up and makes the most of it.

Here's how it goes: the band and Mutt were in the studio recording *Hysteria.* Mutt left the room to drain some energy, as it were, and singer Joe Elliott started fooling around on a guitar. Mutt came back in and said, as the English-accented Elliott recounted in *Entertainment Weekly,* "That's the best 'ook I've heard in five years." The hook became the chorus to "Pour Some Sugar on Me," the centerpiece to an album that sold over fifteen million copies worldwide. "And it was done almost by accident," concludes Elliott. "Had [Mutt] not gone for a piss . . ."

Critics often make mention of the fact that Mutt's hooks sound familiar. A *Rolling Stone* review of *Come on Over* referred to "guitar riffs stolen from 'Spirit in the Sky,' 'La Grange' and 'In the Summertime,' too." It's not unusual for a songwriter to adapt an existing hook, then build a new song out of it. Mutt has a knack for making classic hooks sound fresh, a talent that all the best songwriters share to a degree. By the way, Mutt is also a superb singer, providing smooth background vocals on most of Shania's songs.

"Mutt made the difference. He took these songs, my attitude, my creativity, and colored them in a way that is unique."

—SHANIA

Much has been made of Mutt's rock-and-pop background. What most folks don't know is that his true musical love is country. "He'd like the whole thing to be steel and fiddle," explains Shania. The fact that Mutt has spent decades in one arena shouldn't prevent his entering another. It's all about the love of music, after all. "Mutt is such a big fan of Tammy Wynette and George Jones; he's got such a collection of country music. The steel guitar just makes him want to crank it," Shania once told interviewer Brian Mansfield.

In the spring of 1993 Mutt was living in England. When he was in his studio doing production work, he often had Country Music Television Europe playing in the background. One day Mutt had one eye on the screen when the image of a striking brunette romping on the beach caught his full attention. Of course the video clip he'd seen was for Shania's single "What Made You Say That." His curiosity was aroused. He saw an exceptional talent, perhaps not being used to its fullest capacity, and he had been wanting to dive into country music but was waiting for the right artist to come along.

"Mutt was working out to my album every morning," Shania told Robert K. Oermann. (Mutt's on the far side of forty, but he keeps himself in good shape—and he's an avid fan of soccer.) Calling from London, Mutt got in touch with the folks at Mercury, who put him on to Mary Bailey—who kept him at arm's length. She'd never heard of him. Mutt was more amused than offended when Shania's manager brushed him off. He stuck with his pursuit and eventually got Shania on the line.

He told her who he was, listed a few of the artists he'd worked with. Shania had never noticed his name on the back covers of CDs, but she was familiar with most of the albums Mutt had produced. She was impressed and flattered. It was a sweet gesture for this famous, millionaire producer to go out of his way to contact a new singer whose debut wasn't exactly burning up the charts. He wanted to hear a sample of the songs she'd written, so she sang "Home Ain't Where His Heart Is (Anymore)" over the phone. Mutt reciprocated by playing the song he was working on at the time, "I Said I Loved You but I Lied," which became a hit for pop-soul singer Michael Bolton.

In the weeks that followed, Shania and Mutt spoke often on the phone. The talks were not romantic in nature; Mutt wanted to hear the songs

Shania had been writing. She sang for him over the wires, and on the other end of the line he nodded and smiled to himself. It was going to be a beautiful friendship at the least. They seemed to be in tune with each other on a creative level. "I had already fallen in love with his mind before I ever had any romantic inclinations toward him," Shania has said.

Not long after that initial phone call Mutt and Shania met in person for the first time. To casual observers it must've looked like nothing more than two old friends getting together. No one could have known that, of the thousands of face-to-face first encounters going on around them, this one between Mutt and Shania would have the biggest impact on country music. The place was the Tennessee State Fairgrounds in Nashville, and the event was Fan Fair '93.

Every year since April of 1972 thousands of die-hard country music fans have converged on Music City for a happening unlike any other in the entertainment business. Fan Fair is a big stew of autograph sessions, concerts, parties, and souvenir sales simmering under the hot Southern sun. Upward of 25,000 hard-core country music lovers tie up downtown traffic, stand for hours in chow and autograph lines, and wait for their favorite stars to take a brief turn onstage. Fan Fair can look a lot like a circle of hell to outsiders, but for participants the event is about unconditional love and dedication. Being patient is an ideal means of expressing those virtues, so the inconvenience and discomfort are taken as tests of faith and devotion. In that paradoxical respect, the hassles enhance the experience more than they detract from it.

At the 1993 event Shania was far from the biggest draw. She had no hit singles in her pocket, and a lot of folks might have been hard-pressed to pronounce her name. But even without the throngs of admirers or the attentive media, Shania had a ball. And there was one visitor to her booth who made a big and lasting impression: her new pal, Mutt Lange.

Perhaps the two friends sensed a spark of passion, but at the time their relationship was platonic. Country music was the force that had brought them together, and it was the bond that grew strong between them. It seemed logical for them to collaborate on Shania's next album; the challenge was to find time. Mutt's expertise was in constant demand, and Shania was still trying to build support for *Shania Twain*. She and Mutt continued to ring up fat long-distance bills, crossing paths when their crazy schedules permitted.

In the winter of 1993 Shania and Mutt took a "working trip" to Europe together. Their admiration for each other had only deepened since

THE VH-1 "FIVE DIVAS" BENEFIT CONCERT

Aretha Franklin, Carole King, Shania, and Celine Dion

Celine Dion, Gloria Estefan, and Shania

Shania with Faith Hill . . .

... comparing muscles with Pat Boone

Steve Granitz/Retna Ltd.

... with her dog, Tim

Ron Davis/Shooting Star

Shania in top form at the Country Music Awards

The famous midriff

Very much the lady at the Presidential Gala

that first face-to-face at Fan Fair, and the bond had turned from artistic to romantic. Shania was keeping her feelings for Mutt secret—she wanted to be sure. "Just one day we hugged each other," she said in *Rolling Stone*. "But it was such a—it was a different kind of hug, and that was actually when we knew. . . . It was a very sweet, honest moment." In beautiful Spain the feeling overtook Shania's heart. "Looking at him the day I fell in love," Shania has said of Mutt, "and looking at him the day before? Two different things." When the glowing couple arrived in Paris, Mutt presented Shania with a 2.5-carat diamond ring and asked for her hand in marriage. She said yes without hesitation.

The happy couple couldn't wait to tie the knot, but first Mutt needed to take care of some unfinished business. He sprang for Carrie-Ann and Jill to fly across and explore the celebrated City of Lights with Shania. Then the four of them hopped a plane and headed to Huntsville, Ontario, for a wedding. A few of their friends and family members said they were crazy to jump into marriage so soon after first meeting. Later there was a stream of calls to Shania's management asking if the couple was getting a divorce. The tabloids have also spread rumors to that effect, but Shania stresses that none of them are accurate. "I think the advantage we have together is that we love each other," she once said.

On December 28, 1993, Shania and Mutt took the vows of holy matrimony and became husband and wife. It was the happiest moment of Shania's life, with loved ones all around her and a lifetime of adventure unfolding before her. Shania says she used to feel lost before she met Mutt, but she doesn't feel lost anymore. It makes her smile twice as wide, knowing in her heart that Jerry and Sharon are looking down from heaven and smiling, too.

Shania's personal life had become more fulfilling than she had ever dreamed possible, but her professional life was in crisis. As she and Mutt adjusted to married life, it was time to create the album they believed would breathe new life into Shania's career. If you held the belief that her charisma and creativity had been stifled on *Shania Twain*, the solution was to make this second attempt stand or fall on her talent alone.

In other words, fashion an album that would represent the real Shania rather than just another singer plugged into someone else's musical sensibility. The key was to be Shania's own songwriting, backed by Mutt's know-how. "He's responsible for the sound," Shania was quoted as saying by Jon Bream in *TV Guide*. "But the writing and the attitude are definitely me. It's a real partnership." Most of the song ideas that weren't used on her debut album found their way onto

The Woman in Me. Mutt and Shania had already finished writing half the songs before they got together romantically. After they hooked up, it simply became a perfect union of two great songwriters. "We're a total ma and pa household," Shania told *New Country*. "But we'll write a song that way."

Shania's approach to songwriting is childlike, in the best sense of the word. "Writing's like coloring," she asserts. "Kids like to color, they don't need to have a reason to color—they just like it. They have no inhibitions. They are totally open to being creative. That's how I feel about songwriting. It's a chance to just create without inhibitions." It is a form of expression she has been drawn to since her afternoons alone in the bush as a preteen and later in the Timmins High and Vocational band room. And because she started writing at such a young age (she was ten when she wrote her first song), Shania is less restricted in her approach. What's more, she had roughly twenty years to develop her material for *The Woman in Me*, and with Mutt she was teamed with one of the best songwriters in the universe. As she puts it, they're "a two-guitar family."

Shania explains what Mutt had in mind for *The Woman in Me*: "Right from the beginning he said, 'We need to go into your catalogue. I want to know what you've been writing, then we'll go

from there.' " Most of the basic ideas were ones
Shania had been working on long before she met
Mutt. As in the "Pour Some Sugar on Me" anecdote, Mutt lent his keen ear for hooks and his genius for taking an artist's raw concepts and
fleshing them into perfectly realized songs. But he
wouldn't have been interested in working with
someone who wasn't a songwriter, and Shania
feels the same. "Being a singer of other people's
songs can be very superficial," she contends in a
Dotmusic article. "I wouldn't be willing to take the
risks I do if it didn't all feel like me."

The songwriting process was ongoing. "When-
ever Mutt and I do anything together, we're
always song writing," Shania says. Mutt and
Shania worked on songs over dinner, while
watching TV, during long walks. "We're not
artsy people," Shania insists. "We're everyday
people who like to throw around creative
ideas." The Twain/Lange dual credit can be
found on ten of the twelve compositions on *The
Woman in Me.* "We work well together because we
come from opposite places. We complement
each other," Shania pointed out in a *VUE Weekly*
article by Wendy Boulding.

Mutt is a notorious perfectionist, and Shania is
much the same. He gives her the push and encouragement to work on her songs until they are
polished and sharp. "He sends me away and says
'No, that lyric's not quite there yet.' He's made

me a much better writer," Shania asserts. On the other hand, she won't abandon an idea just because he doesn't take to it right away. There are times when Shania comes up with something that Mutt isn't at all interested in developing, but if she brings up the same idea later, it's possible he'll really be into it. Then again, in some instances Shania will be skeptical about one of her own ideas, but Mutt will reassure her that it's a good one. "I mean, this guy has a brain that's unbelievable," Shania told Bruce Feiler in *Live!* "So when you say something, he computes it into a million things."

Mutt had no intention of producing an album that wasn't up to his exacting standards, and his standards are *exacting*. Looking again at the Def Leppard *Hysteria* album for illustration: The band had begun recording tracks without Mutt because his calendar was booked up, but the process was stopped when drummer Rick Allen's arm had to be amputated after a car accident. Mutt was back at the helm when the band returned to the studio, but he decided to scrap the existing tapes and start from scratch. He knew what he was doing—the sales of *Hysteria* attest loud and clear on this front—but that sort of thing can get expensive.

Based on the modest sales of *Shania Twain*, Mercury-Nashville wasn't anxious to risk picking up the full tab on a such a project. So, prior to entering the studio, Mutt cut an unusual deal with the label. He would cover most of the costs with his own cash, thus buying himself the freedom to produce *The Woman in Me* as he saw fit. The move was no mere flaunting of wealth, nor was it just an indulgence of his new wife. Mutt had faith in Shania's abilities, and he was smart enough to invest in them.

The results were dramatic. It used to be that country music albums were little more than vehicles for singles (that's still true in a lot of cases) but there isn't one throwaway track on *The Woman in Me*. All the songs have hooks piled upon hooks; with most of the tunes you can get a different part stuck in your head each day for a week. (Mutt would later win ASCAP's Songwriter of the Year honor for his work on *The Woman in Me*, plus the hit song "I'm Not Strong Enough to Say No," recorded by the group Blackhawk.)

The production is layered like an onion in a Chinese box, like an Abstract Expressionist canvas that has been painted over, layer upon layer, until the colors seem to flow and throb. The album is great to listen to with headphones. The tempos shift, the moods alter—there isn't a dull or meaningless moment. What's more—you can dance to it! When country dancers at 350 clubs across the U.S. were asked to vote for their favorite album of 1996, *The Woman in Me* was a hands-down winner.

Song for song *The Woman in Me* stacks up as a country music classic:

"Home Ain't Where His Heart Is (Anymore)"

This is a bare-bones ballad of fading love that shows the emotional honesty of Shania's writing. The tone of the lyrics on *The Woman in Me* swings from tender to tough, with this one falling on the softer side. The instrumental intro interweaves steel and acoustic guitar with a plaintive bass line, and the effect is haunting. A velvet-fogged male voice floats behind Shania's in the chorus.

Scenes of domestic discord in the video, directed by Steven Goldmann, reflect the "adult reality" of post–Kris Kristofferson country music. One of the most serious and sad songs in Shania's repertoire, this is the tune Shania sang for Mutt during their first phone conversation. It was also the first one they finished together, demo'd, recorded, and mixed, so it seemed appropriate to lead off the album.

"Any Man of Mine"

Shania doesn't cry in her beer for long, and track two finds her posting ground rules for would-be suitors. Her good humor keeps the song from feeling like man-bashing. The song became an anthem of strength for many young women, but the message was more passive in Shania's first version. A new guitar riff of Mutt's gave the song a new feel, and the words were rewritten in their current form.

The barbershop-quartet-like backing vocals and pseudo-rap line-dance calls are good fun, while the mix of hoedown fiddles, "We Will Rock You" drums, and arena-rock guitars are a kick in the head. This song, the second single from the album, spent a couple of weeks at the top of the *Billboard* country charts in the summer of 1995.

"Whose Bed Have Your Boots Been Under?"

This one was chosen as the first single from *The Woman in Me*, in no small part because it's an up-tempo number that still doesn't push the Nashville envelope too far—not that it didn't ruffle a few feathers. A shuffle beat and plenty of pedal steel and fiddles lend a familiar country flavor, but there is something bubbling under the surface that says, "This is not your grandpa's country music."

As in "Any Man of Mine" and "(If You're Not in It for Love) I'm Outta Here," Shania gives the man in question a witty tweak on the nose. She exposes the pathetic part of his cheating ways by asking, "This time did it feel like thunder?"

"Whose Bed" is another song that Shania had been working on long before she met Mutt. "It's really cool to be able to come up with a hook that someone like Mutt believes in," Shania said. "He feels it's a hit song." And so it was. It debuted on the *Billboard* country chart in March of 1995, peaking at number eleven, and later being certified gold.

"(If You're Not in It for Love) I'm Outta Here"

This tune and the video that accompanied it threw Nashville for a loop. It starts off with a holler from the lungs of a mid-eighties rocker, the midtempo blues guitar line is sleek and strong, and the drums that lead into the chorus are tribal—all of which makes for cool contrast when blended with Shania's sultry vocals. The album's fourth single and its second number-one smash, the song and its accompanying video were a sensation.

No stranger to cheeseball come-ons, Shania skewers the pickup artists and has a fine time doing it. She surely mined her after-show encounters at Deerhurst for lyric material on this one. She pulls off impressive vocal acrobatics, covering two singing parts in the chorus. It reportedly took five hours to get the right fit for the black velvet pants Shania wore for the video.

"The Woman in Me (Needs the Man in You)"

This song drops the pace back a step to the level of "Home Ain't Where His Heart Is (Anymore)." Shania again shows a vulnerable side, confessing, "I'm not always strong." This is one of her most majestic and traditional vocal performances, and the rising chorus is a tour de force. The piano-and-strings fade-out is a lovely touch, hearkening back to the country-pop of the mid-seventies.

The video, which is set in a desert, is one of the most sensual and seductive ever shot. *"The Woman in Me* (Needs the Man in You)" wasn't a huge hit compared with the up-tempo singles from the album, but it did climb to number fourteen on the *Billboard* country chart in the fall of 1995.

"Is There Life After Love?"

This one keeps within the structure of a modern country ballad, but Mutt gives it extra juice with plenty of lush production flourishes. Shania sings about the consequences of her decision to admit an indiscretion to her boyfriend, but the sad and subtle lyrics explore a deeper question: Does love create impossible expectations, and can folks get beyond their disappointment when harsh truths break the spell? Shania might not write like a philosopher or a politician, but in matters of the heart she is perceptive to the point of genius.

"If It Don't Take Two"

A moderate-fast-tempo shuffle, insistent fiddles, and funky guitar stylings forge a strong backbone for this track. It is a terrific song, and only the desire to avoid overkill kept it from being released as a single. Shania's cute lyrics blend romantic images with references to Noah's Ark ("and the animals came two by two") in making a case for togetherness. The "whoaooooo" in the chorus is a masterful hook unto itself, and the all-male backing vocals add texture and spice.

"You Win My Love"

Mutt gets the sole writing credit for this car-as-sexual-metaphor rocker. "You Win My Love" stretches the country envelope to the breaking point, but Shania's twang combined with superb fiddle and pedal steel work to keep the tune on country radio playlists.

The video shows Shania cutting loose on a go-cart track, intercut with racing footage. When she delivers the "classy little chassis" line, it's enough to stop traffic. The song hit the top of the charts for two weeks in March of 1996—a full year after "Whose Bed Have Your Boots Been Under?" became the first *Woman in Me* single to hit the charts.

"Raining on Our Love"

This cut provides further evidence that Shania qualifies as a first-class country crooner. She follows the cheap thrills of "You Win My Love" with genuine heartbreak, a sad tale of good love lost from neglect. Voices drenched in regret, Shania and Mutt harmonize words that are dripping with remorse.

Once again the sweeping strings, acoustic guitar, and pedal steel meld to create an opulent atmosphere around Shania's home truths. If this is the least distinctive song on the album, as some have suggested, that tells you just how special the rest of the songs on *The Woman in Me* really are.

"Leaving Is the Only Way Out"

This is a Patsy Cline–style tearjerker, the story of a loving but strong woman who has reached the end of her patience with a cheating man. The honesty and heart are pure Shania, and Mutt does an understated but stellar job on the production touches. "Leaving Is the Only Way Out" is the only song on the album that is credited to Shania alone.

In general, the more rockin' tunes on *The Woman in Me* have the "this gal ain't gonna take any more crap" lyrics, while the torch songs keep more or less within traditional bounds (lamenting lost love, etc.). Not so "Leaving Is the Only Way Out," in which Shania's voice oozes vulnerability while her words are filled with strength and resolve.

"No One Needs to Know"

Yet another number-one hit, this peppy little shuffle highlights Terry McMillan's harmonica and has the easy-does-it feel of an old flannel shirt. The story, straight from Shania's heart, is about a woman who has fallen in love but isn't ready to confess it to anyone just yet. John Hughey's pedal steel sounds terrific here, as do Mutt's vocal harmonies. The opening sequence of the video gives a neat glimpse of how Shania works on a song with her band. This tune found its way onto the soundtrack of the feature film *Twister*.

"God Bless the Child"

An a cappella lullaby that Shania wrote for herself and her siblings after the death of her parents, this is not a cover of the Billie Holiday standard of the same name. Shania stated in a press release from Mercury-Nashville: "I would go for long walks in the bush by myself with this song swimming around my head . . . When I met Mutt, I sang it for him and he said, 'Wow—that's beautiful!' We didn't even change it. There's no chorus, no verse, just a thought . . ."

❧ 7 ❧

Time for a Cool Change

"In 1996, mainstream country's creative torch
passed from Garth Brooks to Shania Twain."
  —JAMES HUNTER, *New Country*

"I love this girl's singing. And I'd love to do an
album with her. She caught my ear above all the
rest of them."
  —GEORGE JONES on Shania

After all the instrumental and vocal parts were
recorded and the overdubs were added at three
separate Nashville studios, Mutt mixed the finished product in Quebec. When all the studio
work was completed, and the album was "in the
can," nearly a year had passed since the process
began. Shania was sure of one thing: she and Mutt
had created a record that they could be proud of,

no matter what happened in regard to sales. She remembers speculating, "Wouldn't it be exciting if this went platinum?"

There was one other thing of which Mutt and Shania could be certain—if *The Woman in Me* wasn't a success with the public, it wouldn't be because they had cut corners. The reported total expenditures for the album: half a million dollars—roughly five times the cost of the average country album. Some reports have said as much as $700,000. *The Woman in Me* stands as the most expensive album in Nashville history, a piece of trivia that some critics latched onto as evidence that something had gone rotten in Music City. As it turns out, *The Woman in Me* is the *Titanic* (the movie, not the ship) of the country music industry. Expensive, but worth it.

Mark Lepage, a reviewer for Canada's *Country* magazine, foresaw the reaction from some segments of Nashville, noting that Shania could "expect to be greeted with as many smirks as smiles," and that her "drop-dead gorgeous" looks "should bring out the claws in all quarters." Lepage's prediction was right on target, and although the sniping didn't catch Shania by surprise, she had, and still has, to deal with it.

You know the feeling. People are talking behind your back. Maybe they don't even know you, and maybe what they're saying isn't true.

They're jealous, or ignorant, or worse. Either way you don't want to be criticized unfairly, and you don't want other people to be swayed by the lies. Should you confront the critics, ignore them, or try to change yourself to make them happy? Will what you do even make a difference?

A vocal minority of folks in Nashville are downright snippy about Shania. For example, a tidbit in the "People" section of the Jan./Feb. 1998 issue of *Country Music* read: "I hear that Shania Twain is threatening to do a concert this summer at Nashville Arena." And according to Brian D. Johnson in *Maclean's*, musician Steve Earle "once dismissed [Shania] as 'the world's highest paid lap dancer.' " A headline in the *London Times* blared NASHVILLE HATES SHANIA.

The guardians of tradition used to say Shania'd be a flash in the pan. Now they claim she's nothing but the product of her "Svengali" husband/producer. (Svengali is an evil hypnotist in a famous nineteenth-century novel who induces others to do his bidding.) Shania is too classy to lash back at the critics; in fact, she defends Nashville, calling it more open-minded and diverse than it is portrayed. She tries to put on a positive spin: "I feel a new sense of freedom," she proclaims. "I feel I've made my place, and people accept me for who I am."

Of course she also can't help hearing the

negative talk that swirls around in the media, and she sometimes tries to set the record straight. "My whole thing is I want to be myself," she told Nicholas Jennings in *Maclean's*. I don't want to be a product of anything—whether it's a photographer, a makeup artist, a record label or even a producer."

The question of being a "product" might never come up if not for the silly carping of a few uptight elitists. They argue that the fans are being duped, but in reality the critics are just snobs who can't stand to see a woman playing on the outskirts of Music City's creative limits. It's too bad, but the dismissive viewpoint has become an accepted truth in the media. One reviewer wrote, "No one can argue that her packaging, if you'll pardon the euphemism, was the key to her initial success."

A lot of folks still feel, as journalist Bruce Feiler wrote in his book *Dreaming Out Loud*, that the heart of country music is about "a yearning for security, for comfort, for family, for happiness, and, especially in our rootless society, for rootedness." If an artist is going to shake those roots, invade that comfort zone, she's bound to hear some hollerin', as Shania certainly has.

Shania never set out to be a rebel or to ruffle any feathers; her goal is to make good music and entertain people. But she has run up against subtle and not-so-subtle resistance that indicates she's shaking the tree the way an artist is supposed to. She does it with her music, her words, her attitude . . . and yes, her appearance.

It's no revelation to note that Shania is a babe. In an informal survey taken on a national sports talk radio show, Shania was chosen World's Most Beautiful Woman, nosing out supermodel Kathy Ireland in the final vote. When she first came on the scene, some critics were sure that because she had a sexy image, that was all she had. But they were just being shallow, not looking past that revved-up image to the broader appeal of her music.

When the critics say that she's too sexy or too pop, Shania takes the heat with grace. "I'm aware of the criticism, but I don't feel pressure from it," she told journalist Nick Krewen. After all, she is pushing Nashville's envelope. But if country music is to stay vibrant, it has to have fresh blood and new ideas. That means change, and that means diversity. The best artists of each new generation pay tribute to their forebears without merely copying them.

In that respect, it's best for country music to stay flexible and open to the "People Like Shania," as James Hunter dubbed them in *New Country*. New artists such as Mindy McCready, Deana Carter, Jo Dee Messina, Matraca Berg, and Chely Wright, who are, as Hunter puts it, "choosing whatever they like from rock and pop to arrive at an encouraging amount of unfettered new country."

Yet more than any other kind of popular music, country has arguably the deepest sense of tradition and thus is the most skittish about change. A lot of the people who now make up the Nashville establishment used to stir things up when they first came to town. Now the same people are afraid of change; afraid they'll be left in the dust, or just scared that their legacy will be lost.

Remember how Buck Owens put fresh life into country music by mixing it with Chuck Berry–style rock and roll? He may not have seen it this way at the time, but he was giving spark to the idea that country artists could draw from rock's energy and still make great country music. To find a link from old-school country of the forties and fifties to New Country, look no further than Don Rich's fuzztone guitar solo on Buck's 1969 hit "Who's Gonna Mow Your Grass?" Buck has recounted that longtime fans "damn-near lynched" him because of that little experiment.

Nobody today would ever question that Buck is real country—for good reason. We hear in his music only great songwriting and that raw twang. But at the peak of his success he was attacked by the ever-nervous old guard who said he was too rock and roll. In those days Buck was also a Nashville outsider, at odds with the Music City way of doing things. "He detested both their formula approach to making music and their insistence on acting as if Nashville's word was the final word," wrote Rich Kienzle in the liner notes of the Rhino CD *The Very Best of Buck Owens Volume 1.*

Remember the way Shania's first-grade classmates poked fun at her and called her "Twang" when she sang a country song for show-and-tell? You might say that the pint-size school kids were her first critics. In their eyes she was too country. Today the most common attempt at an insult you'll hear about Shania's music is that it's "too pop." As criticism, it runs in the same vein as a roomful of six-year-olds calling her Twang. Shania put it this way to John Sakamoto of *The Toronto Sun:* "But what is pop? I mean, pop goes from Snoop Doggy Dogg to Celine Dion. We're all just people who make music for the purpose of pleasing as many people as we can."

The thing most New Country artists find compelling about pop is that it's the closest you can get to total musical freedom. There is no debate about what is authentic pop because the genre is wide open: literally anything goes, from jazz to blues to classical to hip-hop to folk to punk to country. Modern rock bands such as Son Volt and Virginia Keen infuse traditional country into their sound. Modern country bands do the same with classic rock and pop, dipping into that stew of options while keeping a country base. In doing so, they wind up creating music that is new and refreshing. In these complicated times country isn't easy to define. Garth does some nice Don Ho moves on his hit "Two Piña Coladas." Rock icon Sting sang at the CMA Awards. Anything goes. If the people who like country music buy it, then it must be country.

If being country were a gift of birth—rather than "a frame of mind" (as Shania sees it)—that might rule out Trisha Yearwood, the daughter of a rich banker, or Alison Krauss, who grew up listening to Bad Company, and it would most likely rule out a lot of other great musicians in Nashville. Speaking to the influx of new people with diverse backgrounds, Shania points out, "If you didn't have fresh blood and people who are willing to go to the edge, I think that you do run the risk of having cookie-cutter music."

As the great Reba McEntire said in *Country America*, "Country is not what country was . . . It's a very broad spectrum, and I'm glad of that." And, truth is, change happens whether you're glad about it or not. You can cheer it on or throw rocks at it, but sooner or later it happens either way. In the end there are two ways to respond: either hunker down and resist or stick your neck out and see what might be of use.

✹ 8 ✹

We Like It Like That

"It's gotta be all heart."
—SHANIA, in answer to the question,
"What does impress Shania Twain?"

Despite the initial mixed reviews and concerns about whether fans would accept her, Shania soon found good reason to be optimistic about the future. While the first single from *The Woman in Me*, "Whose Bed Have Your Boots Been Under?", didn't crack *Billboard*'s top ten, it did perform far better than any song off *Shania Twain* had done.

An improved promotional strategy accounts for part of the leap forward. Mercury-Nashville had teamed Shania with John and Bo Derek to orchestrate photo shoots and direct her first two videos. This made good horse sense in light of Shania's natural assets and the visual nature of the modern music business. Shania's midriff is a virtual legend—one writer suggested that it should have its own agent. The tag line for a piece on the entertainment-news show *E!* read: "Shania Twain—Is she too sexy for country?"

It would have been foolish to pretend that images weren't going to be an important part of the publicity for *The Woman in Me.* On the flip side, it's nonsense to assume that a sexy image can prop up an album of songs no one cares about. After all, how many copies of teen babe Jennifer Love Hewitt's three albums have been sold in the U.S.? Shania is well aware that it's the music that counts; as she puts it, "No one's going to care what Shania Twain looks like if the album isn't great."

Country Music Television barely deigned to play the "Whose Bed Have Your Boots Been Under?" video until after the song had become established on radio. Luke Lewis, the president of Mercury-Nashville, explains that while CMT's official position was that the video was too repetitive, the folks at Shania's record label felt the decision had more to do with Shania being seen as "too sexy" by the CMT video selection committee.

In the video in question Shania is inside a rural diner filled with regular guys of all ages eating breakfast. She dances around the room singing the song and poking gentle fun at the oblivious men. She does look alluring in a sleek-fitting burgundy dress, but the sexual content of the video is hardly extreme—it's downright tame compared with the average perfume commercial. CMT's tune changed right quick when the song started to work its way up the charts. These days CMT is a little bit more supportive of Shania. She was the network's Showcase Artist for February of 1996. "She's magic on camera," chief programmer Tracy Rogers was quoted as saying in *TV Guide*. "She's 100 percent babe. But she's talented, too. It's the combination that makes her work."

Shania had been knocking on the door, and now the time was right for her to kick it down. The big boot that did the job was "Any Man of Mine," the second single from *The Woman in Me*. It was the definitive song from the album, the tune that best expressed Shania's attitude and Mutt's influence. "I think this could be the impact song on the album," she announced in a press release.

Was it ever. In fact, "Any Man of Mine" is a modern classic, and not merely because it spent seventeen weeks in the Top 40 and two at number one on the *Billboard* country chart. As a *Time* magazine article put it, "The throaty intimacy, the smart selling of each phrase, the drawl of lightly ironic girls' talk in 'just a little too tight,' her clear but not prissy enunciation—these are the signs of a true storyteller in song." John Derek's rather simple video of Shania as a sexy farmgirl turned a lot of male heads, and it also turned Shania into something of an icon among young female viewers who liked her blend of country charm and city sophistication.

But, again, the song was what mattered. The supercharged hook had everyone singing and dancing along, while the take-me-as-I-am-or-take-a-hike lyrics struck a chord with both guys and gals. In an article by Peter Howell in *The Toronto Star*, Shania explained, "It's really just saying, 'Look, we know nobody's perfect.' Whether you're a guy or a girl, here's a few lyrics to make you laugh at yourself a little bit." Shania recounts a particular anecdote that shows how "Any Man of Mine" touched real people's lives. It seems that one evening a woman who was cooking dinner rushed off to answer the phone, and when she came back the meat was burned to a crisp. Instead of being impatient, her husband said "Mmm, I like it like that . . ." quoting the line from "Any Man of Mine." The wife "was just in tears [of joy]," said Shania, over the husband's reaction.

When the 1995 Fan Fair rolled around in June, Clint Black's hit "Summer's Comin' " was the number-one song on the charts. But it was "Any Man of Mine" that had people talking. It had shot to number four like a bullet—by the end of July it would be positioned in the top spot. Folks at Fan Fair '95 were clamoring to see and meet the woman behind *The Woman in Me*. It was a far cry from her Fan Fair experience of two years earlier, when she felt lucky to have been invited at all.

Now she was the toast of the event—or at least one of its most popular attractions. All manner of Nashville insiders had her name on their lips, and the new fans kept her booth packed throughout the week.

Meanwhile, across the Canadian border in Quebec, *The Woman in Me* became the top-selling album in the province—quite a feat when you consider that the province is Celine Dion's home turf. It was the perfect start to the incredible summer of what Shania later called the best year of her life. In the spring she and Mutt had kicked off the process of assembling a band for doing promotional gigs.

A classified ad in an Albany, New York, newspaper netted guitarist David Malachowski, who'd gotten in touch with Shania's personal assistant, Sheri Thorn. Mutt and Shania had given David charge of putting the rest of the band together. As it turns out, the group was composed of non-Nashville musicians; in fact, most of the players were from rock-and-roll backgrounds.

At the beginning of July director Markus Blunder, a video crew, and Shania were in Egypt to film the clip for the song "The Woman in Me." Shania suffered a painful ankle scrape when the horse she was riding passed too close to one of the pyramids, but the shoot went well and the video itself turned out to be one of the most beautiful ever created.

From there Shania flew to the U.K. for a three-show promotion with her new band. In the city of Glasgow, Scotland, the group did a five-song set that included a cover of "Blue Eyes Cryin' in the Rain." But for that exception, an old Roy Acuff tune that Willie Nelson took to number one back in 1975, Shania and her band stuck with the singles from *The Woman in Me*. For all three U.K. shows, the other two of which were in the English cities of Manchester and London, the venues were small and the crowds consisted of media and record executives.

Two weeks later Shania and her band were booked to jam on *The Tonight Show*. The song of choice, "Any Man of Mine," was sitting on top of *Billboard*'s country singles chart. With that feat, Shania had become the first Canadian in a decade to post a U.S. number one. (The legendary "Snowbird" Anne Murray had scored with "Now and Forever [You and Me]" back in 1986.) Shania unleashed an inspired performance of her new smash hit, while her nine-piece band just about blew the lid off the Burbank studio. Shania's entire entourage felt an ominous rumbling, and it was no L.A. earthquake: *The Woman in Me* was going to be huge.

Two more weeks passed and she was back on national television, this time in New York City for *Live!* with Regis and Kathie Lee. "Any Man of Mine" was again the selection she performed, although this time she did so without the full band. Shania's star was rising, but it was all happening so fast, she hardly had time to catch her breath and enjoy the process. "I think the speed is what overwhelms me more than anything," she told the trade magazine *Network.*

In late August of 1995, as her thirtieth birthday approached, Shania cohosted a music festival at Wonderland, an amusement park just north of Toronto. She had left her band behind, so when the crowd began screaming for her to perform one of her hits, she took the opportunity to exhibit her vocal skills with an a cappella version of "Any Man of Mine." The fans went nuts, and Shania wound up signing autographs and posing for photos, à la Fan Fair, for hours after the show had ended. The next day she was hard at work in a Toronto photo studio, posing for pictures that would later be seen on billboards and at bus stops.

The talk was that Shania would soon be on tour, if not as a headliner, at least opening for an established star or perhaps coheadlining. Neal McCoy, one of the genre's most individual artists (he does a tune called "Hillbilly Rap" that is part "The Ballad of Jed Clampett" and part "Rapper's Delight"), had released a new album, and there was speculation that Shania might go on tour with him. With all due respect to Neal, even more exciting was the possibility of a lucrative tour with

Wynonna Judd. Mary Bailey was working hard to bring it together, and the Shania camp was buzzing.

On the last night of August, Mercury-Nashville put on a showcase concert in Laguna Beach, California. Shania and her band were onstage to begin their set when Luke Lewis announced that Shania had decided not to tour in support of *The Woman in Me*. It was a shock to most of the folks gathered for the event, including Shania's band.

The decision proved to be controversial, and some critics took it as an opportunity to attack. There were whispers that Shania couldn't sing her songs outside of the studio—a ridiculous notion, since she had been doing this very thing throughout the summer (and all of her life, for that matter).

She tried to explain her reasoning to and through the press: the sudden success of *The Woman in Me* caught everyone by surprise. There wasn't time to put together a full show, and an off-the-cuff setup wasn't acceptable. Rather than take a chance on burning out her fans and herself, rather than going on the road with one album's worth of hits, Shania would wait until she had completed her next release to launch her first world tour. She told Kay Richmond of *Country Music International*, "We just want to put together the best live show we can." Seeing it in that light, the choice was rather clear.

Shania wasn't the only artist who felt that fans were being stretched too thin by heavy touring. "People in country music traditionally have toured constantly, and I don't think we're all going to be able to sustain that type of tour," Clint Black told *New Country*. "You're asking a lot of the country concert-goer." Members of the group Blackhawk, for whom Mutt wrote the hit song "I'm Not Strong Enough to Say No," spoke out directly in support of Shania's decision, saying she would "be able to pick and choose when and where she performs."

It was Shania's intent to make sure, as she explained to Mario Tarradell in a *Halifax Daily News* article, that "[the songs] support the show as opposed to the show supporting the songs." In other words, she would tour when the time was right. After that evening in Laguna Beach the news spread through the press that Shania was not going to go on the road in the usual sense, and she was questioned nonstop about the decision. "I felt like I was getting more attention for not touring than if I'd gone out," she told Rick Overall in *The Ottawa Sun*.

"Let's not sell the music. Let the music sell itself," became her standard response. And as journalist John P. McLaughlin wrote in *The Vancouver Province*, "However the gulps must have dominoed around the conference table [at Shania's record label], the woman was right. In a biz where constant live exposure has always been the coin of trade, the music of her *The Woman in Me* album did sell itself. Sort of."

That "sort of" was, of course, no small detail. World tour or no, Shania wasn't sitting at home counting her blessings. September was a whirlwind month: she flew to British Columbia to sing "The Woman in Me (Needs the Man in You)" with the Vancouver Symphony as part of an all-star show that featured fellow Canadians Michelle Wright and Sarah McLachlan, among others. The sold-out auditorium echoed with the approval of 25,000 fans, and Shania left all of them screaming for more.

It had been an amazing year so far, but it wasn't over yet. The awards season was gearing up, and Shania would be taking home her share of the trophies. One of the first groups to honor her was the Canadian Country Music Association, which showered Shania with seven nominations and prizes in five categories, including Female Vocalist of the Year, Album of the Year, and Single of the Year ("Any Man of Mine").

Besides the obvious triumph for Shania, this was also perhaps the crowning moment of Mary Bailey's life in country music. She had helped her protégée to accomplish what neither woman might ever have done alone. Sitting next to Shania in the audience, Mary wept when her friend and client's name was announced, just as she had done years before when little Shania had sung "I'm So Lonesome I Could Cry."

Shania was back in New York City at the start of October, singing "(If You're Not in It for Love) I'm Outta Here" on *Late Night with David Letterman*. The excitement was palpable—people in the media were talking "Shania-mania." Shania was met by crowds of adoring admirers at every turn, and she never failed to reach out to the fans who made her feel so loved. The attention was inspiring; Shania and her band were joined that night by the Letterman house band for one of the most electric of Shania's 1995 promotional performances.

The Woman in Me had gone three times platinum by the first week in November, and it had been on the charts for ten months. If there was a shred of doubt about the sheer scope of Shania-mania in America, it was swept away when she rode on a giant turkey float for the Thanksgiving Day parade in New York. Asked what she'd be wearing for the ride down the avenue, Shania gave an amusing one-word answer: "Thermals."

Earlier that same month she sang for President and Mrs. Clinton at a celebration gala at Ford's Theatre in Washington. Asked how the hectic schedule was affecting her and Mutt, Shania replied, "I've been so busy, we usually pass each other at airports." Of course she had to keep up the pace and take advantage of being "the latest thing" for as long as possible. "You can't just say, 'Oh, let's close the store for a couple of weeks,' " she once said. "People are just going to think you're out of business."

At the *Billboard* Music Awards show in December, Shania and her band performed "I'm Outta Here" live (as opposed to lip-synching as most of the acts did), and just about blew the roof off the New York Coliseum. On a sad note, this was to be the final night of Mary's tenure as manager. She would later be notified that her client and friend Shania was going to move forward without her.

The music business is a high-stakes, cutthroat game. You can't win without bringing your whole heart to the table, but you must also understand that it can be broken into a million pieces. The decision Shania made—to replace Mary Bailey as her manager—was brutal for both of them. It's a tough call to argue against on a business level, but the personal cost was astronomical.

Shania spoke of not getting "caught in a comfort zone," of the need to grow and move forward. There was nothing that Mary could do but accept the situation, express her grief, and wish Shania the best, which she did with class. It would be a long time before a replacement was hired; Jon Landau and Barbara Carr, who also manage Bruce Springsteen and Natalie Merchant, earned

Shania's selection. "I was determined to take a break and decide what it is I really need in a manager, what is going to just make it all come together, which is what a manager does," Shania told *The Halifax Daily News*. With that, she put the past behind her and set her sights on an open future.

As the Christmas season approached, *The Woman in Me* was certified a whopping four times platinum. Shania and Mutt settled in for a holiday celebration at their upstate New York studio apartment, which was home for them until construction was completed on the main residence of their 3,000-acre estate in the woods of the Adirondack Mountains. Located in the town of Saranac Lake, near Lake Placid and just a few hours from New York City, the property is sacred ground for Mutt and Shania.

The atmosphere is haunting and mysterious, with impenetrable forests and forbiddingly cold lakes. Shania is enchanted by the cries of the loons that inhabit the area, and it's no coincidence that the copyrights for the songs on *The Woman in Me* read "Loon Echo Music." Shania and Mutt love to take long walks on the grounds, which include a lake where Shania can canoe, tennis courts, and a horse stable.

One of Shania's deepest passions is horseback riding. It was a childhood dream to own horses, and now she has five: two spotted saddle walkers, a palomino, a miniature, and an Andalusian named Dancer. She rides every day when she's at home, and Dancer has his own trailer so that he can travel with Shania when she's on tour.

It means a lot to Shania to be able to get away from the cameras and be alone in the wilderness. "I spend most of my time with my horses and dogs," she told Michael Bane in *Country Music*, "and they don't care how I look." (In light of Shania's love of nature, and how much the land means to her, it's not hard to see why she was upset when, in late 1996, stories popped up in the press that officials were looking into whether construction of the music studio had violated local zoning laws. Mutt and Shania argued that the building was for "artisan's activities," and therefore didn't need a permit.)

Being home was a welcome respite from the rigors of perpetual travel, but the promotional work didn't grind to a complete stop. An interviewer from *Homemaker's* chronicled the Lange-Twain dinner, sketching a portrait of the loving couple relaxing at home. The article served as a gift to Shania fans looking for an inside glimpse of her private life, which turns out to be not so different from that of most folks. "I'm just a very average, pretty square person," as Shania once put it to Jill Phillips in *Countrybeat.*

That sentiment might seem cheap to someone who can't see past the flash and glamour of stardom, but keep in mind Shania's upbringing and it makes perfect sense. Her nature is such that the part of her that craves isolation is as real as the side that cultivates worldwide attention. As she says, "I'm a chameleon, but when I center myself again, I'm always just plain."

❊ 9 ❊

She Wins Our Love

"As soon as you get to a certain point, it's no longer hip to dig you."
—KRIS KRISTOFFERSON

When the Christmas–New Year's break had passed and 1996 was in full swing, Shania was back on the awards and promotion trail. Far from slowing down, sales of *The Woman in Me* were picking up steam. At the American Music Awards gala in late January she snagged the trophy for Favorite New Country Artist, and her band gave arguably its hottest performance to date in yet another enthusiastic take on "I'm Outta Here." Whether she was doing endorsements for Washburn guitars, chatting on *Oprah*, performing at the National Aboriginal Awards, or opening a new arena in Vancouver, the buzz phrase for Shania was "busy as a bee."

In lieu of a concert tour Shania made public

appearances in Minneapolis, Dallas, Toronto, and Calgary. The events, coined Fan Appreciation Days, were analogous to one-woman Fan Fairs, complete with autographs and photo ops. The concept drew predictable snide commentary from the press: "She's the Mall of America's ideal of what a woman should be: kind, pretty, generous, unthreatening. For four hours, Shania puts all those qualities on sale," wrote Karen Schoemer in *Newsweek.*

That particular event, on November 4, 1997, in Bloomington, Minnesota, at the largest indoor mall in the U.S., drew some 10,000 fans, the vast majority of whom don't care a lick what the media thinks about their ideals. The Minneapolis–St. Paul area is one of the hotbeds of country music fandom in America. People began lining up for Shania's four P.M. autograph session at six-thirty in the morning. Shania told the crowd, "I have no one else to thank but you, the fans. You're fantastic!"

Shania made a return engagement on the Letterman show (singing "You Win My Love") in late February. It had been a full year since *The Woman in Me* had hit the stores, and it stood at a cool five times platinum. Two weeks after the Letterman encore, Shania was voted Favorite New Country Artist by the fans at the Blockbuster Entertainment Awards in L.A., and she again rocked the hall with "You Win My Love," the third number one from *The Woman in Me*.

At the twenty-fifth Juno Awards (the Canadian equivalent of the Grammy Awards) in March, Shania was chosen Country Female Vocalist of the Year and Entertainer of the Year. The latter award was based on a phone-in vote by fans, and it was the lone category in which Shania beat out rocker Alanis Morissette in direct competition. Shania was slated to sing at the event but had to bow out with the flu.

For a while it had seemed the good times would keep flowing unabated, but bad news comes in waves, and a couple of doozies were about to crash onto Shania's beach. The first trouble arose from an unexpected source: Shania's hometown newspaper, *The Timmins Daily Press*. During the spring the paper began printing articles with headlines such as THE FATHER SHANIA TURNED HER BACK ON and SHANIA CONFESSES SHE MIGHT NOT BE NATIVE. The unpleasant situation was summed up in an April 5, 1996, article, under the headline SHANIA TWAIN'S "OTHER" FAMILY CRITICIZES RED-HOT SINGER. The article read in part:

> In a series of stories, the *Timmins Press* reports that Twain's biological grandmother and other unnamed relatives are upset that Nashville's hottest act is no longer in touch with them.

The stories also suggest that she may have oversold her Native heritage . . .

At the peak of her success, after all she had done to honor her parents and fulfill their dream, Shania's personal heritage was being called into question. It seems that reporters from the *Timmins Press* had gotten in touch with the mother of Clarence Edwards (Shania's biological father). She informed the reporters of the Edwards family's existence and insisted that there was no Indian blood in the family.

It is true that Shania wasn't completely up-front about the circumstances of her birth. In the letter to her fans that was published in *Country* in 1994, she stated that her "mother was out of town on a visit to Windsor" when Shania was born there. Shania had tried to keep her origins private, as was her right, but the press, as it so often does, had caught the scent of a secret and blown it into a major scandal. "Half the people in my life didn't know I was adopted," Shania has said. "Why should I have told the press?"

It was really no one's business if Shania didn't want people to know every detail of her past, but once the details came out through the media, she was forced to address the issue in public. She told Fred Schuster of the Los Angeles *Daily News*, "It's ridiculous to have this family try to claim me back. Our struggle ever since my parents died was to stay grounded and anchored as a family. This new development is like a divider. It's kind of late to try and claim me."

In reality, the question of Shania's birth parents' Indian, or non-Indian, descent was moot, because her adoption by Jerry Twain meant that she was "legally registered as 50 percent North American Indian," as she wrote in her statement to the press. She had never lied about a single aspect of her Indian heritage. Sharon, her mother, had told Shania that Clarence was part Indian. If it wasn't accurate, Shania couldn't have known, and in either case, there can be no dispute of her legal and cultural status.

To his credit, Clarence Edwards refused comment to the media. John P. McLaughlin of *The Vancouver Province* wrote, "Relatives and friends in Chapleau, a small lumber community, describe him as a quiet, unassuming man who speaks little of his famous offspring." The *Daily Press* later printed a "clarification" that called the situation "a misunderstanding." The experience was a hurtful one for Shania, and she is still pestered from time to time with queries from reporters about her heritage. "I believe that it's very important that we respect each other and act in a professional manner," she has said of her relationship with the press. Her main concern is to make sure, as she told Jackie Bissley in *Windspeaker*, "that the community, especially the Native youth, understand that I have not lied to them."

The tabloid media, however, wasn't finished with Shania and the Twains, not by a long shot. When Mark and Darryl, both in their twenties and still living in Ontario, were arrested for attempting to break into a Huntsville car dealership, the media made much ado about the fact that a superstar's siblings were in trouble.

It was a difficult time for the family. Shania couldn't help being shocked when she realized that her fame made it profitable for scandal-savvy journalists to inflate the mistakes of her brothers into big news. At the same time Mark and Darryl, who are now working in the bush cutting timber, couldn't help feeling sorry that their famous sister's reputation might be tainted by their actions. "It's difficult for them to be exposed if they do anything wrong," Shania comments, "but at the same time it helps keep them straight." Shania tried to take this sad episode in stride and not get "bitter and twisted," as she put it. "I guess you know you've made a certain level when you make the tabloids," she commented. It's part of the price of fame, however unfair. Often it seems the function of the press is to throw gasoline on little fires.

The media-manufactured brouhaha over her heritage and the tabloid hoopla about her siblings' problems with the law didn't cloud Shania's focus or dampen her enthusiasm for her music and her fans. The summer found her on familiar grounds: the Tennessee State Fairgounds, to be precise. Fan Fair 1996 was one of the best ever. Garth Brooks and Reba McEntire showed up for the first time in a while, and a thirteen-year-old newcomer named LeAnn Rimes made her first appearance. Shania took part in a charity softball game with stars such as Vince Gill and Kix Brooks. It was the twenty-fifth anniversary of Fan Fair, and the mood was electric.

Shania had been to each Fan Fair since 1993, when she had met her future husband Mutt Lange for the first time face-to-face. At the 1995 showing she had belted out three songs from *The Woman in Me*. At that time the album was on the verge of being certified platinum; now it was at seven times that and climbing. No album by a woman in country music history had sold more copies— ever. It was pure elation at the Shania Twain booth for Fan Fair '96, and the best was yet to come.

With so many artists and so many fans to accommodate, attentions tend to be scattered for much of the week. Still there are moments when it seems as if all eyes and ears are on a particular stage at one special moment. The Mercury-Nashville show featured a number of hot artists: Billy Ray Cyrus, Terri Clark, Sammy Kershaw, and Kim Richey. But the headliner was Shania, no question.

Her five-song set of "Any Man of Mine," "Home Ain't Where His Heart Is (Anymore)," "You Win My Love," "No One Needs to Know," and "(If You're Not in It for Love) I'm Outta Here" had the expectant crowd of 20,000-plus singing and dancing. In what was to be her only public concert with a full band all year, Shania's ear monitor malfunctioned just prior to her entry onstage. She did the entire show, in front of thousands of screaming fans, without monitors, a feat that no singer would wish to attempt. Shania kept her cool and pulled through the tricky situation like a trouper.

Shania's live set was the highlight of the week for most of her fans, but for her it took a backseat. Reflecting on the peaks and valleys of her life to this point, just a couple of months from her thirty-first birthday, she felt blessed to be able to create such joy for herself and her fans. Her life was rarely simple, and it wasn't always fun, but the gains far outstripped the losses, and what's more, she could give back to the folks who'd given her so much.

It was in this frame of mind that she attended the Fan Fair events at which disabled fans have exclusive access to their favorite stars. The time she spent meeting with these special fans, a large number of whom were wheelchair-bound, meant as much to her as anything she'd done on her wild ride from rags to riches. The sparkle in their eyes, the warmth of their hugs—this was worth as much as—and maybe more than—all the gold and platinum albums she'd ever earn.

Of course, after the hustle and bustle of Fan Fair, it was crucial for Shania to feed the part of her soul that craves solitude, if only for a few days. Back in the woods of upstate New York, safe from the stresses of Nashville, she tried to relax and get settled into her home. Shania once described her hectic travel pace to writer Marilyn Beck of *The Vancouver Province*: "I don't even unpack," she lamented. "I just switch things in and out." And her suitcases weren't destined for the closet quite yet.

The Woman in Me was running strong on the charts as the summer of '96 progressed. The fifth single, "No One Needs to Know," had become the album's fourth number one, and there was no end in sight. Shania sang the song on Rosie O'Donnell's afternoon talk show in June and again on *Late Night with Conan O'Brien* in late August, the day after her birthday. These various New York City television gigs allowed her to reach her fans without going too far from home. She was thankful for the chance to catch her breath.

The nominations for the Canadian Country Music Awards were announced on August 7, and the results showed that Shania wasn't the only new star in the Great White North. Terri Clark, the young woman from Medicine Hat, Alberta, was named in seven categories, one more than Shania. It's been suggested that the barrier between Canada and Nashville was cracked open by Anne Murray, pushed wider by Michelle Wright, and blown to bits by Shania. Artists such as Terri Clark are now marching into the breach. When the awards were handed out a couple of months later, Shania came away with the coveted Female Vocalist of the Year award and the fan-voted Entertainer of the Year. In her acceptance speech an emotional Shania told the audience, "I just want to say the life of this album has been amazing. I never expected to win this award again."

A week later Shania was in Toronto for another fan appreciation day, this one at the Canadian National Exhibition festival, one of the country's biggest summer events. Shania—the little girl who rode hundreds of miles to the big city for voice lessons, the young woman who had tried to establish her career there only to be pulled away when her parents were killed—had returned a conquering heroine.

More than 6,000 fans turned out to wait in the August heat for their idol, who arrived with her dog, Tim. She picked up the two Junos she'd been too ill to receive in person on the night of the awards, in addition to receiving a Diamond

Award for selling one million records in Canada; she's the first country artist ever to accomplish this feat, and she eventually racked up double that number. That makes for an incredible percentage in a country whose population is under thirty million; it would be roughly parallel to selling *eighteen million* in the U.S.

Not so long ago it would have been just about impossible for Shania to sell such a huge number of records in Canada, for a reason other than the population size: Can-Con, which stands for Canadian Content. An outfit called the CRTC (which is like the FCC in the U.S.) mandates that all Canadian radio stations play a certain percentage (30 percent for AM stations; between 15 and 30 for FM) of Can-Con material.

To be considered Can-Con, a song must be of no less than 50 percent Canadian origin, taking into account music, lyrics, production, and artist(s). A notorious case of an album not being Can-Con was the huge hit *Waking Up the Neighbours*, which was cowritten by Mutt Lange and produced in England, making it not Can-Con even though the artist, Bryan Adams, was a Canadian. After that incident the rules were changed so that a cowritten album, such as *The Woman in Me*, would qualify as Can-Con.

There is another regulation that could have hampered Shania's sales in her own homeland. The CRTC limits the number of hits a station can play. For instance, FM stations can't devote more than 50 percent of their programming to songs that are on the charts (*Billboard* or its Canadian equivalents). This means, in effect, that if an act is good enough to make a big splash on the deep end of success, the CRTC responds by draining half the water from the pool.

Shania's autograph signings at the CNE were limited to just a couple of hundred because she was due in Washington the next day for President Clinton's birthday party. After the signings and photo sessions she answered questions from the audience. A little girl in the crowd had just had a birthday, and Shania sang "Happy Birthday" in her honor. One fan, quoted the next day in *The Toronto Star*, expressed her feelings about Shania, saying, "I like her because ... she never gave up on her dream."

The outpouring of affection in Toronto was intense, but perhaps not quite so poignant as the one just a few days before in Timmins. On August 15, 1996, Shania's hometown had inaugurated Shania Twain Day. Thousands of local citizens and distant visitors, encouraged by the singer's beaming presence, weathered the cold sheets of rain that drenched the festivities. She quipped that it was "a bad hair day" for the entire city (a sly reference to a line from "Any Man of Mine"). The honors bestowed upon the town's favorite daughter included the renaming of a section of street "Shania Twain Way" and the unveiling of a billboard featuring Shania's face as it appears on the cover of *The Woman in Me*. But the best part for Shania was having her grandmother accompany her to the festivities.

She received the key to the city from the mayor, and a beautiful guitar-shaped garden was dedicated in her name. Shania left her handprints in cement as part of the ceremonies, and she planted a tree for her late grandfather and in memory of the business her parents had worked so hard to build. "This is a symbol of replacing some of what we take from nature," she noted during the planting. Shania wished that Sharon and Jerry could have been on hand for the festivities, but she had long since come to terms with their loss. "I never felt that life was over during that time," she once told reporter Peter North. "Time is a great healer and you've got to stop wishing for what will never happen. Mom and Dad will never be here to celebrate my success." There were upward of 4,000 people present at Hollinger Park, and when the crowd sang "Happy Birthday" to her, she sang it right back to them.

That night a gala benefit was held with Shania as belle of the ball, escorted by two men whose upper bodies were painted gold. Black ties and evening gowns were the order of the evening, and a red carpet was rolled out for the guest of honor.

The conductor of the local symphony orchestra presented a special new composition he'd entitled "Shania's Waltz." It was the perfect expression of this once-in-a-lifetime affair. Shania was overwhelmed, saying, "I feel like the same person as when I left town but now I'm treated like a queen." It had been an experience she would never forget.

Halfway through September of 1996 the sales of *The Woman in Me* had reached eight million copies. Despite almost two years on the charts, not to mention being the biggest seller ever by a female artist in country music, the album had yet to generate a single honor from the Country Music Association. The CMAs are perhaps the most coveted awards in the business, and Shania was hopeful that her peers would recognize her accomplishments.

She had been nominated for three CMA Awards in 1995: the Horizon Award (an award for "creative growth"), in addition to Video of the Year and Single of the Year for "Any Man of Mine." When the crystal trophies were handed out, Alison Krauss received both the Horizon and Single of the Year, while the Tractors won in the video category. Although it was a disappointment to go home unrewarded, the album's long chart life would give Shania another chance.

She was up for three more CMA honors in

1996: Female Vocalist of the Year, another Horizon Award, and Song of the Year for "Any Man of Mine." (Single of the Year, for which Mutt and Shania were nominated in '95, goes to the producer and the artist. Song of the Year goes to the songwriter(s), here again being the dynamic duo of Shania and Mutt.) The awards for Song of the Year and Female Vocalist are considered two of the most treasured among CMA honors.

This time the folks at Mercury-Nashville didn't leave much to chance, inundating CMA members with postcards spotlighting Shania's virtues and erecting a large billboard of her not far from Music Row. According to Mitchell Fink in *People* magazine, one CMA member said, "It's the most aggressive campaign I've ever seen coming out of Nashville."

The level of anticipation was high in the Mercury-Nashville camp, but hopes were tempered by an understanding that some CMA members were not open to *The Woman in Me* or its creators. There were those who thought of Shania as the new Olivia Newton-John, the Australian singer who had several crossover hits in the seventies. Newton-John had won Female Vocalist of the Year in 1975, and some CMA members quit in protest. (In a strange side note, an Olivia Newton-John record was certified gold in 1976. The title: *Come on Over*, identical to Shania's third album.)

The Woman in Me was nearing the end of its

phenomenal run, and this was to be the CMA's last opportunity to put its stamp of acceptance on one of the landmark albums in the history of country music. Mercury-Nashville was making certain that CMA members who might choose to ignore the album's success knew precisely what they were dismissing—an album of which the fans had given their absolute approval.

Shania went to the October awards presentation unescorted, as Mutt avoids the limelight at all costs. "He's a very humble guy and basically doesn't want to be a star. He just wants to be a person who makes the music," Shania explained after the show. Mutt's photo almost never appears in the press, and he is rarely interviewed. He's often presented in the press as a mad recluse and/or "power behind the throne." "The mystery that surrounds him has contributed to his reputation," Shania explains.

Shania gave a stirring performance of "God Bless the Child," accompanied by Take 6, but besides having no Mutt to hold her hand when arriving at the 1996 CMA Awards, she also departed the event empty-handed. Song of the Year went to Vince Gill, Best Female Vocalist to Patty Loveless, and the Horizon Award to Bryan White. All the winners were worthy and deserving, but it was absurd that Shania didn't win a single honor for *The Woman in Me*. With six nominations in two years—none for Album of the Year on a release that had been a virtual hit machine—zero trophies smelled as peculiar as an abandoned chicken shed.

Reba McEntire summed up what a lot of people thought about the subject when she told David Zimmerman of *USA Today*: "And when we get a Shania Twain, let's nominate her for Album of the Year, for Pete's sake ... They should have been shouting from the rooftops about what this woman has done in country music ... What does she have to do? ... It's almost like everybody is jealous of her success and I don't like that." Amen, Reba.

Of course Shania doesn't have the time for sour grapes. And in any case her mantel is overflowing with the fruits of recognition. She has won no fewer than twenty-five awards from all corners of the music world. When she wins she credits her parents and all the people who helped her along the way, and when she loses it just motivates her to keep working hard.

October brought good news about some hard work Shania had done in the past. Many of the new fans who'd discovered her through *The Woman in Me* had gone back to record stores to check out *Shania Twain*. Her self-titled debut album had managed to inch its way to gold status after four years in print. It was a reminder of the incredible difference between where her career had been and

where it had gone. Shania had been a virtual unknown in her own country just a couple of years
before; now she was in Australia doing radio
spots and TV interviews to promote her album,
which was burning up the charts down under.

In late November of '96 the final single from
The Woman in Me was released. What made it most
special was the original meaning of the song itself
and the new purpose Shania and Mutt had given
it. "God Bless the Child" is the lullaby that Shania
wrote for herself and her siblings after the accident that took Jerry and Sharon. Mutt and Shania
left the song in its original form on the album, but
for the single they wrote new verses, added instrumentation, and expanded the song into a plea
for suffering children everywhere.

The new version, recorded in a gospel style
(à la Garth's "We Shall Be Free"), featured the
group Take 6, Fisk University's Jubilee Singers,
and the Blair Music School's children's choir. All
proceeds were donated to charities such as the
Second Harvest/Kids' Café and the Canadian Living Foundation, which provide meals for underprivileged children. The song didn't burn up the
U.S. charts—it entered at number seventy-four
and peaked at number forty-eight—but it debuted at number one in Canada and raised thousands of dollars to help feed hungry children.

In one respect, it wasn't the obvious pick for
the final single of the album—"If It Don't Take

Two" would perhaps have had a better shot at hitting number one in the U.S.—but "God Bless the Child" was an ideal choice for bringing a sense of closure and of coming full circle. The success of *The Woman in Me* had been a dream come true for Shania, but the song "God Bless the Child" was her anchor to her past, to the harsh reality of child poverty, and to the imperative that she not forget the hard road she'd traveled and the poor children who were still walking that road.

Christmas was just around the corner, and so was Shania and Mutt's third wedding anniversary. It was going to be the best holiday ever. Shania is a big fan of Mariah Carey's *Merry Christmas* album, and Tammy Wynette's holiday record, too. "I put them on when I'm cooking. It doesn't matter what time of year," she once told Bruce Feiler in *Live!* magazine. The time had come for Mutt and Shania to take stock of the album they had created together, which was nothing less than a country music phenomenon, and to look toward the future.

✳ 10 ✳

She's Still the One

"She works her butt off. She's very results oriented, no-nonsense. And, to me, she is utterly real."

—JON LANDAU

How do you follow perfection? Or, to be more precise, what can an artist do after she has created a masterpiece? The cliché is all too true: a songwriter has an entire life to write that first album and just a few months to write the second. Having spent the better part of three years promoting *The Woman in Me*, which was her debut in all but a literal sense, Shania was excited to get on with the next creative project.

Excited and nervous. Although she tried not to let it affect her work, Shania couldn't help but be aware of the pressure and of the expectations that were riding on her follow-up effort. She was also getting psyched up for her first tour, though that was still a year or so away. Taking a cue from the rock world, she had produced an entire album of great songs and taken them as far as she could for as long as possible. The interim gave her time to work up fresh material for the follow-up album, and she had made the most of the lag time. Shania felt that she had plenty to say after her experiences of the past couple of years. She had evolved, and her songwriting had followed suit.

If anything, her worries were more about the health of country music in general. The genre accounted for over 18 percent of album sales back in 1993, but the number had dipped to around 14 percent in 1996. Even though the industry was raking in a cool $2 billion per annum, there was talk of how the gains that had been made were being lost. Shania was concerned: Would there still be an audience for her when she returned?

But when Garth Brooks scored a huge success with a free concert that drew hundreds of thousands to New York City's Central Park, Shania was energized. If the momentum was rising again, she was prepared to make a major contribution. If the fans were still into what she had to offer, she wanted nothing more than to make it worth their while. When the time came to reenter the studio, Shania had a stomach full of butterflies and a powerful determination to make a record she'd be proud of, one that would top *The Woman in Me* in artistry if not in sales. "It's really up to the artist to come up with something that's original enough for people to believe in you and get behind you," she told *The Toronto Sun*.

She and Mutt had been working in a vacuum, writing songs that were being heard only by each other. They believed something good was happening, but there was no way to be sure. "You never know how the fans are going to respond, but that's the risk that you take. You can't make compromises for those sorts of things; you just have to do what you do," she explained to writer Michael Bane in *Country Music*. The first sign that all was well came from the musicians in the studio. Sure, they were being paid to be there, but they weren't being paid extra for reacting with such enthusiasm to the songs. Shania was relieved and happy, but the real test was still to come; how would the fans respond?

From the title, *Come on Over,* to the feel and subject matter of the songs, the third Shania album is both a personal statement and a fans' record. The gap is small between the person Shania is and the impression of her that emerges on *Come on Over*. If the best way to get to know artists is through their art, then this album is a great way to get to know Shania. It isn't a critics' record, thank goodness. "I like to use phrases people use everyday," explained Shania. "I wanted this album to be conversational. The lyrics are not going to get you an

'A' in grammar, that's for sure. But it's more the way we speak in everyday life."

As with *The Woman in Me*, Mutt and Shania had complete creative control of *Come on Over*. At sixteen songs and about an hour of running time, this is definitely a full-length affair. "There was so much that I wanted to achieve. I couldn't have done it in any less than sixteen songs—every one of them makes this album feel complete to me," she explains. More than twenty-five musicians contributed to the album, including guest vocalist Bryan White. As with its predecessor, *Come on Over* doesn't have a weak track:

"Man! I Feel Like a Woman!"

When a song has two exclamation points in its title, you expect it to be a fun one, and "Man! I Feel Like a Woman" delivers! It's got a foot-stompin' backbeat, juicy guitar hooks that are part "Spirit in the Sky" and part "La Grange," fiddles that really bite, plus Shania's kick-out-the-jambs vocal style. She opens her live shows with this tune.

But it isn't just fluff—there's a message here, too. The song is a celebration of freedom in an age in which women can command respect but still let their hair down if they choose. Shania is feeling liberated and wants to enjoy it. Only a fool would try to stand in her way.

"I'm Holdin' On to Love (to Save My Life)"

The title says sentimental ballad, but this tune is an infectious and feisty romp, full of hand claps and attitude. The lyrics seem to be aimed at those who may have doubted that Mutt and Shania's marriage would last. A pledge of eternal love for the nineties, Shania makes reference to psychics, psychiatrists, the Internet, Dr. Ruth, and evolution ("ain't no missing link").

This was reportedly the toughest song to finish, taking the longest to write and undergoing the most melodic changes. The result came out great, obviously, and it turned out to be a favorite among Shania's family and friends. As always, Shania delivers her point of view with a dash of humor.

"Love Gets Me Every Time"

This was the first single from *Come on Over*. It was nearly titled "Gol' Darn Gone and Done It," but Shania decided that the radio DJs would be stumbling over their own tongues trying to say it. It's a playfully sung Shania gem about how Cupid has a way of targeting your heart when you least expect it. Mutt laughed when he first heard the original title, and Shania took that as a signal that the song was headed in the right direction. The "photo shoot" video gives a nice glimpse of Shania's style and personality (plus we get to see her eat a banana).

"Don't Be Stupid (You Know I Love You)"

This upbeat tune started out simply with Shania's idea to write a song called "Don't Be Stupid." Mutt added the second part of the title later on; a neat twist, turning a harsh reprimand into a reassurance of love, but the sentiments are far more spunky than sappy. Shania won't cotton to a man who doesn't trust her, and you can bet that there'll be a few women out there playing this one for their possessive boyfriends. The song has a vaguely Celtic feel and lends itself nicely to Riverdancing, as the video aptly shows.

"From This Moment On"

Shania's songwriting wheels never stop turning, and this song was written in unusual circumstances—in the midst of a cheering crowd of thousands. "We were in Italy two years ago, and we were at a soccer game," she told *Country Weekly*. "My husband loves sports. I don't know the game that well, so my mind drifted and I started writing."

Asked once whom she would most like to do a duet with, Shania answered, "Elton John would be my first choice." But when the idea arose for making the song a duet, Bryan White came to mind right away. Shania and Bryan sound like they're singing the love theme to a movie soundtrack; in fact, Shania intended it to be sung by a "powerhouse" vocalist, someone like Celine Dion or Bette Midler.

Mutt called Bryan at his tour bus and "auditioned" him over the phone. In a *New Country* interview with Deborah Barnes, Bryan recalled, "And I hadn't been awake very long, so Mutt would say, 'Now sing that back to me,' and I sounded terrible but I'd sing it back to him. And he kept saying, 'Yeah, it's gonna be cool.'" Bryan traveled out to Shania and Mutt's home in the Adirondacks; Bryan and Shania rode horses and got acquainted, and Bryan picked Mutt's brain about various aspects of the music biz, and thus a hit song was created.

"Come on Over"

This song is one of Shania's personal favorites. "I just love the song to death," she enthused to interviewer Rick Overall. It has an uplifting yet easygoing feel; the Latin percussion, accordion, and mandolin give this tune a quirky diversity and a Cajun sound. Shania says this song just makes her happy, and her joy shines through in the vocals.

"When"

This is a Beatlesesque tune with terrific guitar work and a driving *ker-chunka-chunk* feel. The bittersweet humor of the lyrics shows a maturity and subtlety. Shania wrote the words while riding in the car with Mutt, and the process took just a couple of hours from start to finish. That guitar break in the middle is one of the high points of the album's instrumentation, and Mutt's utter brilliance in the studio comes through loud and clear.

"Whatever You Do! Don't!"

Shania is feeling vulnerable, so don't push her over the edge. This mid-tempo song features a plaintive pedal steel in the chorus and gritty fiddles in the verses backing Shania's heartfelt vocals. This is one of the few tunes on the album that finishes with a fade-out. The song builds and builds toward a chorus of release, and Shania's voice rises to meet the challenge.

"If You Want to Touch Her, Ask!"

The guitar lines have a funky-stroll feel, and the vocal hook from Shania's delivery of "start" and "heart" is addictive. The male chorus adds muscle, and Shania tests the upper range of her voice to good effect toward the end of the song. Shania asserts that the lyrics contain a serious message about how important it is to be respectful of personal space. "It's about appealing to the sensitive side, and not being a jerk by just grabbing somebody," she says. She knows how it feels to receive unwelcome touches from over-zealous men, and she wants guys to know that there's a better way. "It's all about respect," she told *Entertainment Weekly*.

"You're Still the One"

Shania's most fully realized crossover single, this song was in heavy rotation on VH1 and Adult

Contemporary radio for months. Like many great songs, it feels as if it has been around forever, yet it's also fresh and exciting—the type of hit that makes you run out and buy an entire album.

The romantic lyrics are a touching tribute to Shania and Mutt's successful marriage. They came from different countries and different musical and economic backgrounds; some people said they'd never last as a couple. But they're still in love, and "You're Still the One" is a testament to that fact.

The black-and-white video, featuring Shania on the beach with a male model, was one of the summer's most popular clips. A mini-CD of dance mixes was put out by Mercury, with titles such as "Soul Solution Percapella Dance Mix" and "Kano Dub."

"Honey I'm Home"

With its "We Will Rock You" drums and down-to-earth words, this song is the grown-up older sister to the *Woman in Me* hit "Any Man of Mine." The character in "Honey I'm Home" isn't looking to get swept off her feet—she's just asking for a foot rub and a cold beer. This is definitely a working woman's anthem.

There might not be a more stark fusion of

power pop and country than the transition from verses to chorus in "Honey I'm Home." The interplay of fiddles and guitars is intense and a little disorienting.

"That Don't Impress Me Much"

She may not think of herself as an actress, but Shania has a flair for breathing life into lyrics with her unique delivery. That playful sense of humor shines through, and Shania manages to let the air out of the male ego without sounding like she hates men. She isn't impressed by mere cleverness, good looks, or material things—it's all about heart to Shania. This is one of Mutt's more interesting musical arrangements, with strong guitar interplay and entertaining backing vocals.

"Black Eyes, Blue Tears"

This song covers a serious subject—domestic abuse—and Shania's perspective is both supportive and proactive: simply put, you deserve better, so be strong and move on. Shania has referenced the movie *Thelma and Louise* in relation to "Black Eyes, Blue Tears." She doesn't go for "drive off a cliff" endings—find your self-esteem and walk away free is her advice. In terms of the music, you won't find talk-box guitar solos (à la Peter Frampton) on most country albums, but Mutt pulls it off here.

"I Won't Leave You Lonely"

A gently rocking duet between Mutt and Shania, the rhythm track may remind you of the Police classic "Every Breath You Take." The juxtaposing of accordions and pedal steel again works to perfection, lending a European flavor. When Shania sings in French and Spanish . . . wow. The song seeps into the veins and makes you want to do something romantic.

"Rock This Country"

The title has multiple meanings, with both "rock" and "country" doing double duty. The pounding beats, sawing fiddles, and sing-along chorus may make critics debate whether to label it rock or country—the pulsing intro does sound a lot like the opening to Foreigner's "Long, Long Way from Home"—but the bottom line is that you can crank it in the car, and it also makes a great concert finale.

"You've Got a Way"

Shania wrote the words to this song two years earlier, when Mutt was working on a Michael Bolton record; in fact, she was upstairs at the soulful crooner's house. Shania has said that this is one of her two or three favorite songs on the album. Spanish-style guitars and gentle brush-work on the drums set the mood, and Shania's lovely vocals bring it all to light.

❧ 11 ❧

Rockin' the Country

"Shania Twain has carved out her own place in country . . . She's playing by her own rules. And she's changing the audience."
—CHET FLIPPO, Nashville correspondent for *Billboard* magazine

Come on Over hit the U.S. stores on November 4, 1997, but the first single, "Love Gets Me Every Time," had made a major impact weeks before. It entered the *Billboard* country chart in October at number four, and in less than a month it hit the top spot. A few country radio stations felt the song was too rock and refused to play it. Such moves don't make sense to Shania, who feels she's been "a good friend to country radio" and vice versa. Despite the minor controversy, the "gol' darn gone and done it" song was too fun and in-spired not to be a smash with the fans. It went gold in the U.S. in just five weeks.

Come on Over sold over 50,000 copies in its first week on the shelves, debuting at number two on the *Billboard* chart for all genres, and was certified three times platinum just three months after its release. Of course it debuted at number one on the country album chart, and it was still at number three a full eight months after release (number eight for all genres). The numbers didn't lie; *Come on Over* was an unconditional hit with the fans, absolute proof that *The Woman in Me* was no fluke.

> "I don't get offended at their analysis of the whole thing, but it always offends me when people take the liberty to knock you. . . . It's not necessarily me personally, but I get offended when people do that with the arts, because it's like, this isn't a race. . . . How can you judge?"
> —SHANIA on critics

Shania and Mutt had turned their artistry up a notch, and the critics were left baffled again. Reviews were mixed at best. A critic in *Stereo Review* called Shania "country's most overrated female" and made comments such as, "There's a youthful mindlessness about the album . . ." Most writers scorned Shania's use of exclamation points in the song titles, and a dismissive tone was de rigueur. "Almost every high-gloss song opens with a bubblegum-glam cheerleader shout, then blasts into radio-ready rapture with offhand vocal interjections," blathered a *Rolling Stone* reviewer.

The review in *Country Music* couched each compliment in a put-down ("Mutt and Shania are indeed the possessors of a genius that's as narrow and calculating as it is appealing"), then suggested that *Come on Over* was best suited for the ears of a ten-year-old. (That might be true, as a child is more apt to listen with an open heart instead of a critic's closed mind.) A reviewer for the Newark *Star–Ledger* sneered: "If you think of country music as a delicatessen, *Come on Over* is pretty much a big hunk of cheese." The review of *Come on Over* at the Music Central Online Web site gave the album one out of five stars, calling it "a bouncy collection of simplistic songs that approach love with an innocence that comes across as not genuine."

A journalist in *Spin* wrote, "Though the boogie-rich, technoid *Come on Over* out-funs any country album in years, to call it a 'radical progression' insults Brooks & Dunn ..." Again, the critic must temper each positive with a negative. You might think that a "boogie-rich" album that "out-funs any country album in years" would stand on its own merits. Instead it draws a specious comparison.

The negative reaction tells more about the state of modern music criticism than it does about

Shania's album. (Most of the great musicians of the past who are now revered by modern critics were also the most popular artists of their time, from Elvis to Hank. If an artist is loved by the public, it takes critics decades to recognize what the great unwashed grasped from the start.) Truth be told, in the dark and skewed world of music reviewers, it just isn't hip to revere Shania, any more than it would be for a teenage wannabe iconoclast to say nice things about the most popular girl in class, the girl who puts her gifts to use with hard work, while the critic sits on the sidelines and makes cutting comments. It's kind of pathetic when you think about it.

Of course, not all music journalists think like this, thank goodness. Robert K. Oermann, who has been called the dean of Nashville music writers, has said of Shania, "There's some grit there. She has a kind of steely determination about her. She's the girl in your high school class that got straight A's not because she was the most gifted, but because she studied really, really hard. And I like her for it." This is a person who has met and spoken with Shania, unlike most reviewers.

Perhaps the nastiest criticism came from a *Toronto Star* critic, who used words such as "contrived" and "nauseating" in a review that was completely unpolluted by objectivity. The writer was in a lather over Shania's supposedly "unenlightened views on what it means to be a feminist," citing a comment Shania made in *Billboard*: "I think we're kind of spoiled in a lot of ways, with the advantages we have," Shania was quoted as saying. "Feminists may not feel that way, but I do. It's pretty darn fun to be a woman."

As for Shania's gender politics, she refuses to play down her femininity, as certain critics would have her do. "I think a lot of what's being stripped from us these days [has to do with the idea] that we need to be more masculine to fit in the world. And that pressure is not coming from men. That pressure is coming from women," Shania has asserted. "I'm not going to put a paper bag over my head and start dressing like a man just so that I'm taken seriously," she told Rachel Charm in *Music Press*.

Shania's brand of liberation is more humanist than feminist—equal parts Miss Kitty from *Gunsmoke* and Dolly Parton in *9-to-5*, with perhaps a dash of *Ally McBeal*. "A lot of the songs on this album say a lot more than what it may seem on the first listen," Shania told a *Baltimore Sun* reporter. "They are from a woman's perspective, but not coming from an angry feminist. I think there's a point where you can take it too far, and when you're taking it too far is when you're angry about it."

Shania's viewpoint is exemplified in the equal partnership she has with her husband and in the balance she maintains between her life and career. She insists, "I won't neglect my personal life. I wouldn't be able to write the songs or play the music, or even be a responsible artist in any way, shape or form if I'm not happy as a person. So my personal life comes first." At the same time Mutt understands that his wife has to do what she has to do to make the most of her career, so he supports her efforts to the best of his ability. "Creatively, romantically, it's a wonderful, wonderful marriage," Shania explains. "My husband Mutt is the producer of my dreams and the love of my life. They are two separate entities, but at the same time what more could any girl ask for?"

There are many people who think of Shania as the perfect example of a strong, modern woman. She works hard, calls her own shots, lives life to the fullest, gets along with all types of folks, and doesn't hide her feminine side. The idea that beauty, brains, and talent can't coexist in the same woman is as old as jealousy itself. Shania once told the Canadian music magazine *Country* that the negative reactions "show me that we still have a long way to go as women. I don't mind proving myself, but I refuse to downplay my looks."

When she talks about "no inhibitions," she means not taking other people's inhibitions and imposing them on herself. Shania would never, for example, do a film scene with nudity or explicit sexuality. She once turned down a non-nude interview with *Penthouse* in the belief that her fans might not want to see her in that type of magazine. She won't do a kissing scene, and the idea of even being seen in a bra or bikini gives her pause. "I'm actually quite shy about certain things like that," Shania confesses. There might seem to be a contradiction in her position—being reticent to flaunt her figure and, at the same time, refusing to pretend she doesn't have one. But it comes clear when you consider the internal struggle for self-definition that most women face. Shania defines her own parameters, and the critics can take it or leave it.

> "I used to be very insecure about having large breasts . . . So now I've decided, 'You know what, no. I'm going to feel comfortable with my breasts.' If they want to look at me as a sex object . . . that's not going to make me crawl into a corner."
> —SHANIA

It might be hard to imagine Shania with a body-image problem, but she certainly has her share of insecurities, just like anyone else. She doesn't like to walk on the beach without a wrap, and she never wears short skirts (even though she sings about doing just that in "Man! I Feel Like a Woman!"). Much of the discomfort stems from her youth. She was athletic, a bit of a tomboy, so when her body began to develop in other ways ("I was running on the football team bouncing!") she tried to cover up.

Shania withdrew even more when immature boys began to force their attentions on her (a subject she covers in-depth in "If You Want to Touch Her, Ask!"). "And that stuff made me want to withdraw from being a girl," she explained in *The Calgary Sun*. As an adult she has learned to be less inhibited about her body and less reticent about dressing however she wants to: "I'm going to move the way I like to move," she told Anika Van Wyk. "I'm not going to do it in a potato sack."

For the release of *Come on Over*, the promo blitz was extensive, just as you'd expect. There were life-size cardboard cutouts of Shania in record stores, and she glad-handed radio execs at Planet Hollywood in Nashville. It's all part of the game, as Shania knows, but her take on such things isn't at all cynical; she considers it "nice" that folks want to meet and greet her. Shania once told Wray Ellis of *Country Wave*, "I think the best advice anyone could ever give me, and I get advice from left, right and center, is ... humility." Shania treats the press with respect, and she never takes the attention for granted.

She made a stop on *The Tonight Show* in the first week after *Come on Over* came out, and she also appeared at a couple of fan appreciation days. Shania visited Calgary, where a reported 27,000 fans packed into Southcentre Mall. Besides signing autographs and posing for pictures, she also met one of her most special fans, a three-year-old named Alexander McDonald. The little boy had been in a coma after inhaling smoke during a house fire, and doctors said his condition was unlikely to improve. But according to his mother, Alex "started rolling around and kicking his feet" after hearing Shania on the radio. At the fan appreciation event Alex greeted Shania with a Winnie the Pooh cup. "This is the most fun part of my job," Shania professed.

At one point Shania went into the crowd to hug the people who were wheelchair-bound. One disabled fan decided to hold on a little longer than usual, but Shania didn't pull away. She also met and kissed dozens of babies and received hundreds of flowers and gifts from admirers. She didn't take breaks and stayed at the mall far beyond the scheduled time to make sure everyone who wanted an autograph got one. Later she got word that *The Woman in Me* had been certified ten times platinum in the U.S., as Shania joined Garth Brooks, Kenny Rogers, Wynonna Judd, and LeAnn Rimes as the only country artists ever to reach the ten-million-sold (U.S.) plateau with one album.

December brought more fantastic news. After a string of television talk-show dates, the nominations were released for the American Music Awards. She was up for Favorite Country Female Performer for the second straight year, although this time, when the winners were called in January, she wasn't among them.

In late February, she and her band were in Nashville for a taping of TNN's *Prime Time Country*, doing four songs from *Come on Over*. The show had gone all out for her appearance: they counted down the days till her arrival by adding pieces to a giant jigsaw puzzle of her (of course, the belly button was the last piece). Her performance was dead on, but later she would comment, "I'm never at my best on television. There's a row of cameras between you and the audience, and it's very weird, very confusing." She didn't look too confused while wielding a chain saw in a log-cutting contest with the show's host—Shania left her opponent in the sawdust.

At the 1998 Juno Awards in March, she took the prize for Country Female Vocalist for the second year in a row. She was in the running for Female Vocalist and Album of the Year but lost both to Sarah McLachlan. She also sang her newest single, "You're Still the One," which has turned out to be her biggest hit to date.

There was a lag of about four months from the

album's debut in America and its first appearance on U.K. store shelves. In that span, Mutt and Shania went back into the studio to further tweak some of the songs. "We didn't want to change the whole record outside the U.S., just make it a little better," Shania was quoted by Ian Nicolson in *Dotmusic*. While the first two U.S. singles were "Love Gets Me Every Time" and "Don't Be Stupid (You Know I Love You)," the first two U.K. singles were "You're Still the One" and "When." For obvious reasons, country music has a stronger fan base in America than abroad; the international focus is more on the pop aspect of Shania's music. Not only was the non-U.S. version of *Come on Over* remixed and resequenced (the steel guitars and fiddles are more subtle), the cover was changed, too, from the familiar bright red and white to a muted blue-gray. Also, the hit song "From this Moment On," a duet with Bryan White, is sung solo by Shania on the international *Come on Over*. She has recorded duet versions of the song with Irish singer Ronan Keating and the Brazilian duo Chitãozinho E Xororó.

No matter what else Shania is doing, childrens' charities are always on her front burner. In addition to her ongoing work with the Kids' Café/ Second Harvest programs, Shania performed at a UNICEF (United Nations International Children's Emergency Fund) benefit in December, and in April she took part in VHI's Save the Music benefit—*Divas Live!*—to fund music programs in public schools.

The event took place at the Beacon Theater in New York City and featured short sets by Mariah Carey, Gloria Estefan, Celine Dion, Aretha Franklin, and Shania. Her sit-down performance of "You're Still the One" was one of the night's purest moments. That performance was a prelude to the two huge Shania "happenings" to come: the incredible success of "You're Still the One" and the world tour Shania would undertake to support *Come on Over.*

Shania wasn't at all unfamiliar with how it feels to have a number-one single, but a song like "You're Still the One" might come along once in a career. It made an inauspicious chart debut at the bottom (number seventy-five) of the *Billboard* country singles list on January 24, 1998. The video started popping up infrequently on VHI, a rare occurrence for a country artist, to say the least, and an intimation of the cross-genre potential of the song. On the second of May it hit the top spot on the genre chart, but that was just the tip of the iceberg. In the following two months it grew to be one of the most requested videos on VHI, and it reached the number-one position on *Billboard's* Adult Contemporary chart. In short, "You're Still the One" was shaping up to be one of the biggest hits of the summer of '98, regardless of genre. The stage was set for Shania to take it on the road.

"I pick up musicians along the way to do one-off performances, so it's never as good as I want it to be. That really bothers me. So far no one has seen me perform to my full capacity. I can't wait to show people, 'Wait, this is really what I'm like.'"

—SHANIA, prior to kicking off
her first world tour

Because such a fuss had been made over her decision not to tour to support *The Woman in Me*, Shania was motivated to set the record straight—and prove the doubters wrong. "I've just never toured in a luxury bus before," she told *Billboard* in reference to the lean times she'd spent touring as a youngster and with the Triple Play promo tour.

As for luxury buses, Shania stipulated the design for her tour bus, making certain that it had a large kitchen area for her to cook in, plus a private space so she could get plenty of rest between shows. The bus is also set up so that her dog Tim, a German shepherd, can exit easily through his own special door. The important thing for Shania is that the space feel cozy like home, not opulent like a palace.

Shania wanted a young, energetic band behind her. She insists that there be no drug taking and minimal or no alcohol consumption. Shania doesn't smoke (she has mentioned that although she took part in powwows while growing up, she never smoked a peace pipe). In short, she lives "clean" and expects the same of her band. The nine-member group—a different lineup from her prior promo tour—features recruits from places as far apart as Nashville, Chicago, Canada, and Australia.

Shania and her band rehearse until they have each element of the show running like clockwork. That allows them to relax and play their hearts out without having to worry what the other nine people onstage are going to do next. She likens the preparation process to that of studying for an exam in school, and she has compared the concert logistics to putting on a wedding. "I'm glad I waited," she said of the decision not to tour for *The Woman in Me*, "and I'm going to give it all I've got to make it everything the fans have been waiting for."

The tour opened May 29 in Canada, with three nights at Sudbury Arena. By the tenth of June, Shania was on the West Coast of America. From there she worked her way across the U.S. In Detroit, across the river from where she was born, Shania sold out the Pine Knob Amphitheater in under half an hour, on pace with the Who, Metallica, Bob Seger, and Jimmy Buffett. Gigs in Europe, the Far East, and Australia were in the offing, with the tour scheduled to run through the summer of 1999. She puts on a phenomenal show, performing more than twenty songs from her three albums. "I'm very energetic, very athletic, a party animal on stage," she asserts. The music comes first for Shania, but that doesn't prevent her from giving the audience extra entertainment for their concert dollars. Highlights include:

- Shania sitting down to "get comfortable" at center stage, singing an emotional medley of "Home Ain't Where His Heart Is (Anymore")/ "The Woman in Me"/ "You've Got a Way."

- A rollicking version of "Don't Be Stupid" in which Shania is joined onstage by her opening band, Leahy, whose members do a Riverdance and provide extra fiddles.

- An inspired rendition of "Black Eyes, Blue Tears," followed by "God Bless the Child" sung with the choir from a local high school.

- A young girl from the audience coming onstage to sing a duet of "When" with Shania.

- A teen singer, who won a local talent contest, singing "What Made You Say That" solo, with Shania standing by to provide support and backing vocals.

- All the women in the audience dancing and singing "Honey I'm Home" (especially the "This could be worse than P.M.S." line) and "Any Man of Mine," confirming that these tunes are anthems of independence for Shania's legions of female fans.

- Shania's encore, featuring a knockout combo of "From This Moment On," which she does minus the male part, and "I'm Outta Here," at the end of which she jumps through a giant drum and disappears under the stage. When she pops out a minute later, she is hoisted onto a dais and carried through the crowd to shake hands with every person within reach. Then it's back to the stage for a reprise of "Any Man of Mine" and a "Rock This Country" finale.

✻ 12 ✻

Always on Her Way

"I don't have to be a star for the rest of my life to be content. I don't need that much attention. I just want to do music, be appreciated for what I do."

—SHANIA

So, what does the future hold for Shania Twain? If all goes according to plan, she'll be on tour almost until the year 2000, and by then it will no doubt be time to begin production of a new album. She and Mutt have said that there is a good chance they'll purchase a house in Switzerland. That doesn't mean she's planning to abandon her fans in America and Canada, but Shania is well on her way to international superstardom, a goal she's had from the start. She's become quite popular in Australia, the U.K., and the Netherlands, where she's spent a great deal of time and effort on promotions, and she is committed to expanding her international fan base.

There has been speculation that Shania will take a stab at film acting in the future, but she doesn't seem driven to make the leap soon. "I'm not an actress, I can't act," she was quoted as saying by Peter North of *The Edmonton Journal* in a 1995 article. "Maybe the potential is there but it's not in the plans right now." She once spoke of not wanting the visual aspect of her career to overpower the music, saying, "Otherwise, I'd just have become an actress or something." It's been reported that Shania turned down a role opposite Al Pacino, but she has said she'd have to consider any offer that involved Jodie Foster, an actress/director she admires. "It's never really been my goal to become an actress. If I ever do choose to do a movie I'd want to make sure I was good at it," she told James Muretich in *The Calgary Herald*. There is no question that Shania could hold her own as an actress if she put her mind to it, but for now she is sticking to her passion: music.

The magic inherent in Shania's adopted name is that wherever she goes and whatever she does, she'll always be on her way, no doubt to someplace unexpected and beautiful. As she once explained: "Life will dictate itself and unfold. Go with the flow! When you're really desperate, you say a few prayers and hope for the best. That's the way I've always lived my life."

APPENDIX I

Awards

"I can't believe I made it up here. Wow. I hope
I'm holding this the right way."
—SHANIA after winning
a 1995 American Music Award

Academy of Country Music Awards

1995   Album of the Year [*The Woman in Me*]
1995   Top New Female Vocalist

American Music Awards

1995   Favorite New Country Artist
1996   Favorite Country Female Performer

Canadian Country Music Association Awards

1995   Video of the Year ["Any Man of Mine"]
1995   SOCAN* Song of the Year ["Whose Bed
       Have Your Boots Been Under?"]
1995   Single of the Year ["Any Man of Mine"]
1995   Album of the Year [*The Woman in Me*]
1995   Female Vocalist of the Year
1996   Fans' Choice Entertainer of the Year
1996   Video of the Year ["(If You're Not in It for
       Love) I'm Outta Here"]
1996   Female Vocalist of the Year

Country Music Television Europe

1993   Rising Star Award
1995   Video of the Year ["Any Man of Mine"]
1995   Female Artist of the Year

Grammy Awards

1995   Best Country Album [*The Woman in Me*]

*Society of Composers, Authors, and Music Publishers of Canada

Juno Awards

1995 Entertainer of the Year
1995 Country Female Vocalist of the Year
1996 International Achievement Award
1996 Country Female Vocalist of the Year
1997 Country Female Vocalist of the Year

APPENDIX II

Discography

Albums

- *Shania Twain* [1993]
- *The Woman in Me* [1995]
- *Come on Over* [1997]

Singles

- "What Made You Say That" [1993]
- "Dance with the One That Brought You" [1993]
- "You Lay a Whole Lot of Love on Me" [1993]
- "Whose Bed Have Your Boots Been Under?" [1995]
- "Any Man of Mine" [1995]
- "The Woman in Me (Needs the Man in You)" [1995]
- "(If You're Not in It for Love) I'm Outta Here" [1995]
- "You Win My Love" [1996]
- "No One Needs to Know" [1996]

- "Home Ain't Where His Heart Is (Anymore)" [1996]
- "God Bless the Child" [1996]
- "Love Gets Me Every Time" [1997]
- "Don't Be Stupid (You Know I Love You)" [1997]
- "You're Still the One" [1998]
- "From This Moment On" [1998]
- "When" [1998]

Videos

- *The Woman in Me*
- *The Complete Woman in Me Video Collection*

APPENDIX III

Personal Data

"I'm not eccentric. Well, maybe just a little."
—SHANIA

BORN: August 28, 1965, Windsor, Ontario

BIRTH NAME: Eileen Regina Edwards

RAISED: Timmins, Ontario

PARENTS: Jerry Twain (1947–1987) and Sharon Twain (1945–1987); biological father Clarence Edwards

HERITAGE: Irish- and French-Canadian; raised in Ojibwa Indian culture, legally registered 50 percent Ojibwa

SIBLINGS: Jill, Carrie-Ann, Mark, Darryl

HEIGHT: 5' 4"

WEIGHT: 110 lbs

SHOE SIZE: 6 1/2

EYE COLOR: Green

JOBS: McDonald's; foreperson of reforestation crew; administrative assistant at a computer school

IDEAL JOB OTHER THAN THE ONE SHE ALREADY HAS: Veterinarian

MARITAL STATUS: Married Robert John "Mutt" Lange, December 28, 1993, Huntsville, Ontario

PET NAMES: Shania calls Mutt "Love"; Mutt calls Shania "Woody" (one of her hairstyles reminds him of the cartoon character)

INSTRUMENT: Acoustic guitar

FAVORITE CITY: Rome, Italy

FAVORITE FOOD: Pasta

FAVORITE DESSERT: Peach Pie

FAVORITE ANIMALS: Horses, dogs, loons

FAVORITE ACTRESSES: Jodie Foster, Jessica Lange

FAVORITE COUNTRY SINGER: Dolly Parton

FAVORITE POP SINGER: Elton John

FAVORITE PASTIMES: Horseback riding, camping

UNUSUAL TALENT: Juggling

*Read on for an excerpt
from the new biography by*

Richard Crouse

A VOICE AND A DREAM
The Celine Dion Story

It was in La Tuque, a small village in Quebec, Canada, in the summer of 1944 that Thérèse Tanguay and Adhemar Dion met and fell in love. Both had grown up in Sainte Anne-des-Monts, a farming village in Quebec's Gaspé region. Following Catholic mores, both had come from sizable families. Adhemar was the eldest of five boys and two girls, while Thérèse was the sixth child of nine.

Fate didn't bring them together until harsh economic times forced both families to relocate to the more thriving La Tuque. One night at a community dance the two joined in an improvised music jam. Thérèse began playing "Le Reel de Sainte Anne," a popular Quebec folk song. Adhemar, who had aspirations to be a musician, accompanied her on accordion. The music swelled, and dancers swirled around them, but they hardly noticed. For the eighteen-year-old Thérèse and twenty-two-year-old Adhemar it was love at first sight. They began courting that night, and a scant ten months later they were married in a Catholic ceremony at the local church.

Although the newlyweds' earliest days had the luster

of a fairy tale—the whirlwind romance, weekends spent playing music with their close friends and family—the young couple's first years were marred by financial woes. After the birth of their first child, Dénise, in August 1946, Adhemar struggled to keep food on the table. As with many Catholic Quebeckers, the children kept coming, and although each new birth was a joyous event, the pressure to support the family mounted. By the mid-1950s the couple had four children with another on the way. Adhemar had run out of options for work in La Tuque and was forced to leave town to find work. He found a good job in Charlemagne, working in a factory, which offered lots of overtime. Putting in eighteen-hour days, he was able to make ends meet.

The town of Charlemagne is situated just twenty miles east of Montreal. A small town with a population bubbling just under 6,000 souls, it lacks the sophisticated urban feel of its neighboring metropolis. A full 90 percent of the working-class town's inhabitants are of French origin; 95 percent of them natives of Quebec. A Canadian government study reports that 98 percent of the population count French as their only language, while only one percent of the townfolk are bilingual—able to speak both English and French. As in most working-class environments, the men do the heavy work—construction and manual labor; the women toil at clerical and service jobs.

The family lived in a tiny rented apartment, the five kids sharing a room, Adhemar never home, always at the factory. Late at night when he finally returned he was often too tired to spend time with his brood, often falling asleep without eating. Thérèse longed for the farm life they had known until the move to Charle-magne—the wide-open space, the simple way of life.

The two conceived a plan to save money to buy a farm. Every day Adhemar saved bus fare by walking to and from the job at the factory. He was so committed to the scheme that even Quebec's cruel winters wouldn't stop him from making the trek on foot. At the end of each day he would give Thérèse the forty cents he had saved by not taking a round trip on the bus. She stowed the coins the old-fashioned way—in a cookie jar.

It took time, but the determined couple saved enough to make a $400 payment on a small piece of land in Charlemagne. Now they had to build a house. With no extra money to hire carpenters, the resourceful couple decided to do the construction work themselves.

Since Celine has become famous, the story of the family home's construction has become part of Quebec's folklore. Adhemar kept up the punishing pace of eighteen-hour days at the factory, building the house in his off-hours. Often he slept for only two or three hours a night, working on the house until four or five A.M., just hours before he had to go to the factory. It was Thérèse, however, who set tongues wagging in the small community. By this time she was pregnant with their seventh child, but that didn't stop her from wielding a hammer, banging nails in the roof of the partially built house.

"Never once did my mother let her pregnancies get in the way of her responsibilities or the needs of her family," Celine says with obvious admiration in her voice. Through sheer strength of will, and the determination to move their family out of the squalor of the small rented apartment, Thérèse and Adhemar built the house from the ground up, even installing the heating system!

The finished home was a busy place. Seven kids, the oldest just nine years old, kept Thérèse busy while Adhemar worked at the factory. Once the kids had been fed and put to bed, she worked at turning the house into a home. Her flair for decorating on a budget soon turned the new home into a comfortable place for family and friends alike. On Friday and Saturday nights the place would ring with music as friends brought over fiddles, drums, and guitars to jam with the tuneful Dion family. Each child was gifted musically, with mellifluous voices that would soar over the din of the acoustic instruments.

Meanwhile the children kept coming. By March 1968, the couple was supporting thirteen offspring—in chronological order, Dénise, Clément, Claudette, Liette, Michel, Louise, Jacques, Daniel, Ghislaine, Linda, Manon, Paul, and Pauline—with another on the way. On March 30, 1968, at 12:30 A.M., just ten days after Thérèse's forty-first birthday, she gave birth to her fourteenth child, a girl she named after a popular song on the Quebec hit parade, "Celine."

The future singing superstar was the largest of Thérèse's children, weighing in at eight pounds, eight ounces at birth. As was only fitting for a little girl who would one day become pop-music royalty, the French-Canadian Genealogical Society reports that Celine is a direct descendant of French Emperor Charlemagne, who ruled from A.D. 768 to 814.

Scholars from the Genealogical Society also claim to have proof that many Quebeckers, including Celine, are descendants of Catherine Baillon. A member of French provincial nobility, Baillon arrived in Quebec City in 1669 as a *fille du roi* (king's woman). These *filles du roi* were women sent to Quebec as spouses for the colonists. Baillon was just one of more than a thousand women who arrived in the French colony between 1665 and 1673. She married Jacques Mirville Deschenes in 1669, a coupling that produced numerous children.

Ballion's lineage goes back twenty-nine generations, all the way to Bernard, once king of Italy, who died in 815. Bernard was the grandson of Charlemagne, the king of the Franks, who was crowned emperor by the pope on Christmas Day in the year 800.

"These kinds of studies bring to the fore the noble side of Quebec society," says the president of the Genealogical Society, Normand Robert.

The young Celine quickly became the darling of the family, doted on by her siblings. Eldest sister Dénise took on a large part of the parenting duty, and to this day still refers to Celine as "my baby."

"While Mom did lunch or things like that, we'd take care of her," says Celine's brother Michel, now acting as her assistant tour director. "I was in a rock-and-roll band, and I'd bring Celine to gigs with me."

Even with the rigors of raising fourteen children, the oldest twenty-two, the youngest an infant, music remained a central part of life in the Dion household. The weekend jam sessions at the Dion house were now a Charlemagne tradition. With the success of these musical evenings in mind Thérèse and Adhemar formed a group with the children to perform at weddings and parties. It was an extension of the weekend jams but brought in extra money to feed and clothe the kids.

Enveloped by such talent, it was natural that Celine would sing almost before she could talk. Her first word was "Dan," a reference to her older brother Daniel, who spent countless hours playing with her. At nine months she spoke her first sentence, *"Maman, je t'aime"* ("Mom, I love you."). After that there was no stopping her. She absorbed the French language very quickly, often able to memorize the entire lyrics to songs at a very young age.

By age four, with the tutoring of her siblings, she was mimicking the singers and dancers she saw at the weekend parties and on television. Her sister Claudette remembers her singing into a spoon or a fork, pretending it was a microphone. Celine's sisters often adorned her in a pretty frock, applied some makeup, and let her perform, using the kitchen table as a stage. The supportive family would gather round, filling the room with rapturous applause after each tune.

The songs Celine sang were mostly Quebec folk melodies, and while her pronunciation of the difficult French words wasn't letter perfect, she had perfect pitch and could hold a tune. A wide smile would cross her face when she sang, and the joy she felt was immediately passed on to anyone who heard her. Her mother says she knew Celine was destined to become a musician from an early age because of her skill at making "people smile and forget their problems."

Celine made her public debut singing at her brother Michel's wedding in 1973. She was just five years old but brought the house down singing three songs, including Roger Whittaker's hit "Mammy Blue." She captured everybody's heart, letting her natural five-octave-range voice fill the church. Her family was in awe of her talent even then. "It was at that point we realized she would become a famous singer," says Claudette. For Celine, the wedding and a subsequent concert at the La Cachette hotel in Joliette confirmed her desire to become a performer.

Life in the Dion house was idyllic for young Celine. Surrounded by her protective siblings, parents, and beloved collection of dolls—fourteen in all, one for each of the Dion kids—it was a happy, safe place. The outside world was a little less kind. When she was just five years old a terrifying accident rocked the Dion home.

Celine was playing on the street in front of her house as her father and brother Clément worked in the yard. Spying a baby carriage across the street, Celine made a beeline for it. She loved playing with babies and wanted to see what was inside the carriage. She crossed the street despite her mother's warnings never to venture into the road alone. On the other side of the street the baby's mother yelled for Celine to stop, but it was too late. Realizing she had broken her promise to her mother never to go in the street, she froze, unsure what to do. Just then a delivery truck backed into the street. The driver, unaware that a little girl was standing in the road, hit her, tossing her in the air. Celine landed with a thud on her head, knocked unconscious.

Michel, who was in the house at the time of the accident, heard the ruckus and ran out to investigate. He knew Celine was out-of-doors, and prayed that nothing had happened to her. His worst fears were confirmed as he saw his youngest sister lying motionless on the road.

He scooped her up in his arms, rushing her to the hospital. Doctors told the family Celine had severely fractured her skull, warning that she might not fully recover. Two long days passed as she lay still in the intensive-care unit. The family held a round-the-clock vigil at the hospital, weeping and praying for her to recover. Claudette later called those days the "most devastating time in our lives."

Perhaps it was the resilient nature of her young body, but Celine recuperated with no physical damage. Other, later traumas were emotional not physical, but no less hurtful. Leaving the confines of the house to enter school, Celine encountered relentless teasing from her classmates. They called her "the vampire" because of her pronounced front teeth. These taunts were very painful to the young girl, who retreated to the comfort of her family rather than make new friends at school.

**Published by Ballantine Books.
Available in bookstores everywhere.**